TRANSPORTATION ISSUES, POLICIES AND R&D

TRAFFIC ACCIDENTS AND SAFETY

NEW RESEARCH

TRANSPORTATION ISSUES, POLICIES AND R&D

Additional books in this series can be found on Nova's website under the Series tab.

Additional e-books in this series can be found on Nova's website under the e-book tab.

TRANSPORTATION ISSUES, POLICIES AND R&D

TRAFFIC ACCIDENTS AND SAFETY

NEW RESEARCH

GARRETT BOWMAN
EDITOR

New York

Library of Congress Cataloging-in-Publication Data

Names: Bowman, Garrett, editor.
Title: Traffic accidents and safety: new research / editor, Garrett Bowman.
Other titles: Transportation issues, policies and R&D series.
Description: Hauppauge, New York: Nova Science Publishers, Inc., [2016] |
Series: Transportation issues, policies and R&D | Includes index.
Identifiers: LCCN 2016023909 (print) | LCCN 2016034263 (ebook) | ISBN 9781634855174 (softcover) |
ISBN 9781634855549 ()
Subjects: LCSH: Traffic accidents--Psychological aspects. | Traffic accidents--Health aspects. |
Motorcycling accidents. | Traffic safety. |
Motor vehicle driving. | Post-traumatic stress disorder.
Classification: LCC HE5614 .T6847 2016 (print) | LCC HE5614 (ebook) | DDC 363.12/5--dc23
LC record available at https://lccn.loc.gov/2016023909

Published by Nova Science Publishers, Inc. † New York

Contents

PREFACE

Traffic accidents (TAs) represent a significant public health issue and are associated with behavioral factors, vehicles safeties and conditions of the urban spaces. According to the Centers for Disease Control and Prevention, road crashes are one of the major causes of morbidity and mortality in the United States. There are many studies showing that children and adolescents may suffer significant and long-lasting psychosocial consequences following TAs. Countless research has been conducted during the last decades aiming to investigate the relationship between driver behavior and road features. This book provides new research on traffic accidents and safety.

Chapter 1 - Traffic accidents (TAs) are a leading cause of morbidity and mortality among children and adolescents in industrialized countries. There are many studies showing that children and adolescents may suffer significant and long-lasting psychosocial consequences following TAs. Most studies indicate that the prevalence of posttraumatic stress symptoms (PTSS)/disorder (PTSD) among children and adolescents is 12-46% in the first 4 months and 13-25% 4-12 months following TAs. Traffic accidents are also related to acute stress disorder (ASD), mood disorders, development of fears and negative impact on health related quality of life (HRQoL).

Although PTSD (sometimes with delayed onset) may significantly impede young people's development causing substantial subjective distress and resulting in impaired functioning, physicians often ignore or underestimate the likelihood of PTSD development and they are unaware of risk factors that predict its development and future persistence. Therefore young victims' psychological needs often remain unrecognized and unmet.

Most studies suggest that gender but not age is related to development of PTSD among children and adolescents following TAs. Findings regarding type of accident as a risk factor have been inconsistent. The severity of body injury has been found to be unrelated to pediatric PTSD after TAs. However, the occurrence of brain injury after TAs has been reported to be correlated with PTSS, with mild brain injury predicting a higher risk of PTSD compared to no brain injury. Parental PTSS/PTSD, depression, endorsement of worry, and general family functioning have been found to increase the risk of developing PTSD among children.

Maladaptive appraisals have been associated with the development and maintenance of pediatric PTSD after TAs, whereas other cognitive processes, such as subjective threat and memory processes, have been shown to have a possible effect only in the acute phase.

In addition, initial biological responses to trauma as reflected by immediate posttraumatic alterations in neuroendocrine and/or inflammatory factors—increased plasma noradrenaline concentrations, increased or decreased cortisol levels, and increased serumIL-6 concentrations, increased urinary cortisol and epinephrine levels —have also been reported to be involved in subsequent PTSD development in children and adolescents.

Systematic screening of the potential psychological impact (peri-traumatic distress, ASD, post-traumatic stress symptoms, depression, anxiety, and other psychological symptoms) of TAs should receive the same priority as screening for physical injury, regardless of injury severity. Active management and referral for treatment as well as identification of children at risk and prevention of PTSD and other psychosocial consequences are also important. More studies of the psychobiology of physical trauma and PTSD in this pediatric population are needed.

Chapter 2 - Traffic accidents represent a significant public health issue and are associated with behavioral factors, vehicles safeties and conditions of the urban spaces.

Some studies characterizing the profile of accidents and their victims have pointed motorcycles as the most cited means of transportation.

The morbidity and mortality due to traffic accidents, is extremely high around the world. However, the proportion of deaths and injuries from motorcycle accidents is particularly high, often a result of higher exposure, a disregard of traffic laws and adoption of risk behaviors.

The social and health impact caused by traffic accidents has been extensively studied, since the hospitalization rate of accident victims is an indicator of the severity of the accidents and can be used to monitor trends and to quantify the event that represents a cost to health services, due to the high percentage of hospital admissions and high hospital care costs.

Strategies should be implemented to propose prevention and control of traffic accidents, also specifically directed to motorcyclists.

Chapter 3 - Countless research has been conducted during the last decades aiming to investigate the relationship between driver behavior and road features. The majority of the research is focused on passenger car speed, even though other modes of transport, for instance motorcycles, may be differently affected. In most of the cases researchers used pneumatic road tubes and video cameras to record vehicles' driving speeds and their vertical position. However, both pose risks to data validity due to human error and the inevitable effect of the equipment to drivers' behavior. The present investigation aims to bridge these gaps by evaluating motorcyclist's behavior and introducing a new methodology based on Global Positioning System (GPS). More specifically, the research is focused on the impact of curvature and road access to riding performance. Within the context of approaching riders' behavior, field measurements were conducted on two-lane rural roads with the use of instrumented with GPS equipment motorcycles. The planning of the experiments took into account various factors that potentially influence the driving behavior e.g., riding experience and presence of pillion. The conclusions drawn provide evidence that the riders' trajectory is correlated with the radius and the length of the curves and riding behavior is affected by the presence or not of a pillion. Finally, strong indications suggest that speed offences adjacent to junctions are more typical for experienced riders compared to inexperienced ones.

Chapter 4 - According to the Centers for Disease Control and Prevention, road crashes are one of the major causes of morbidity and mortality in the United States. The Healthy People 2020 has indicated that accidents are a major public health issue. Most motor-vehicle related events resulting in injury, disability, or death are predictable and preventable. Injuries are the leading cause of death for Americans aged 1 to 44 years and a leading cause of disability for all ages, regardless of sex, race/ethnicity, or socioeconomic status. Although motorcycles represent approximately 3% of all registered vehicles in the United States, motorcycling accounts for more than 13% of highway traffic fatalities. While fatalities normally represent a small percent of other motor vehicle occupants, fatalities can be as high as 40% for the motorcyclists when involved in accidents (or traffic crashes as typically referred to by transportation safety professionals). Motorcyclists are more vulnerable in crashes due to their lack of protection like enclosed vehicles do to motor vehicle occupants, so they are more likely to be severely injured or killed. Therefore, there is a motivation among stakeholders to decrease the injury severity of motorcyclists. A clear understanding of the factors influencing injury severity levels due to motorcycle crashes and the related evidence prevention strategies is of paramount importance. When examining a topic of motorcycle injury severity, it is important to keep into consideration of different issues that include the definition and concept of injury severity, trends in motorcycle crashes, motorcycle-related policies and laws, knowledge of risk and protective factors. The main purpose of this chapter is to discuss the risk factors and protective factors related to injury severity of motorcycle crashes in the US. Important aspects related to motorcycle crashes' injury severity such as methodological challenges related to conceptual clarity and measurement are discussed. In addition, implications for education, research, practice and policy including laws and enforcement are highlighted so that the overall motorcycle safety situation could be improved.

In: Traffic Accidents and Safety: New Research ISBN: 978-1-63485-517-4
Editor: Garrett Bowman

Chapter 1

TRAFFIC ACCIDENTS: EPIDEMIOLOGY, RISK FACTORS, PSYCHOSOCIAL AND NEUROENDOCRINE IMPACT ON CHILDREN AND ADOLESCENTS

***G. Kolaitis*[1], *P. Pervanidou*[2], *G. Giannakopoulos*[1] *and G. P. Chrousos*[2]**

[1]Department of Child Psychiatry, National and Kapodistrian University of Athens, Aghia Sophia Children's Hospital, Greece

[2]First Department of Pediatrics, National and Kapodistrian University of Athens, Aghia Sophia Children's Hospital, Greece

ABSTRACT

Traffic accidents (TAs) are a leading cause of morbidity and mortality among children and adolescents in industrialized countries. There are many studies showing that children and adolescents may suffer significant and long-lasting psychosocial consequences following TAs. Most studies indicate that the prevalence of posttraumatic stress symptoms (PTSS)/disorder (PTSD) among children and adolescents is 12-46% in the first 4 months and 13-25% 4-12 months following TAs. Traffic accidents are also related to acute stress disorder (ASD), mood disorders, development of fears and negative impact on health related quality of life (HRQoL).

Although PTSD (sometimes with delayed onset) may significantly impede young people's development causing substantial subjective distress and resulting in impaired functioning, physicians often ignore or underestimate the likelihood of PTSD development and they are unaware of risk factors that predict its development and future persistence. Therefore young victims' psychological needs often remain unrecognized and unmet.

Most studies suggest that gender but not age is related to development of PTSD among children and adolescents following TAs. Findings regarding type of accident as a risk factor have been inconsistent. The severity of body injury has been found to be unrelated to pediatric PTSD after TAs. However, the occurrence of brain injury after TAs has been reported to be correlated with PTSS, with mild brain injury predicting a higher risk of PTSD compared to no brain injury. Parental PTSS/PTSD, depression, endorsement of worry, and general family functioning have been found to increase the risk of developing PTSD among children.

Maladaptive appraisals have been associated with the development and maintenance of pediatric PTSD after TAs, whereas other cognitive processes, such as subjective threat and memory processes, have been shown to have a possible effect only in the acute phase.

In addition, initial biological responses to trauma as reflected by immediate posttraumatic alterations in neuroendocrine and/or inflammatory factors—increased plasma noradrenaline concentrations, increased or decreased cortisol levels, and increased serumIL-6 concentrations, increased urinary cortisol and epinephrine levels —have also been reported to be involved in subsequent PTSD development in children and adolescents.

Systematic screening of the potential psychological impact (peri-traumatic distress, ASD, post-traumatic stress symptoms, depression, anxiety, and other psychological symptoms) of TAs should receive the same priority as screening for physical injury, regardless of injury severity. Active management and referral for treatment as well as identification of children at risk and prevention of PTSD and other psychosocial consequences are also important. More studies of the psychobiology of physical trauma and PTSD in this pediatric population are needed.

INTRODUCTION

Traffic accidents are a leading cause of morbidity, disability and mortality among young people, aged 15–29 years in industrialized countries. Globally, TAs resulted in 1,2 million deaths and 50 million injuries across the age range during 2002. The burden of disease attributed to road safety is comparable with malaria and tuberculosis. The global burden of tuberculosis is increasing at a rate of 1% per year, while the global burden of TA injuries is predicted to increase by more than 65% by 2020 (Commission for Global Road Safety 2006).

Car deaths on Europe's roads have halved over the last decade, but campaigners say tougher EU laws could prevent many more people from dying needlessly. Ninety percent of the world's fatalities on the roads occur in low- and middle-income countries, even though these countries have approximately half of the world's vehicles. Half of those dying on the world's roads are "vulnerable road users": pedestrians, cyclists and motorcyclists. The newly adopted 2030 Agenda for Sustainable Development's has set an ambitious road safety target of halving the global number of deaths and injuries from road traffic crashes by 2020. Without interventions, TAs will rank third between all causes of morbidity and mortality globally by 2020 (Peden et al. 2004).

Traffic Accidents and Impact on Mental Health

Children and adolescents may suffer significant and long-lasting psychosocial consequences following TAs. Traffic accidents are related to development of post-traumatic stress symptoms (PTSS) and disorder (PTSD), acute stress disorder (ASD), mood disorders, travel anxiety, specific phobias, alcohol abuse; they may also have a negative impact on young victims' health related quality of life (HRQoL). The psychological consequences for parents of children have also been documented (e.g., Kassam-Adams 2009). Nevertheless, less than half of the parents of affected children sought help of any form (including from friends) for their child and only 20% of affected parents sought help for themselves (De Vries et al. 1999).

Development of PTSD and Its Prevalence

Most studies indicate that PTSD is relatively common among children and adolescents following RTAs. Its prevalence varies between studies due to various reasons (e.g., different methodologies used, time since the accident, measures used, definitions), but it is estimated to be between 12-46% in the first 4 months and 13-25% 4-12 months after the TA (Kolaitis et al. 2011, Landolt et al. 2005, Mehta and Ameratunga 2012, Mirza et al. 1998, Olofsson et al. 2009, Pervanidou et al. 2007a, Stallard et al. 2004). Although PTSD, sometimes with a delayed onset, may significantly impede young people's normal development, causing substantial subjective distress and impaired functioning, physicians often ignore or underestimate the likelihood of PTSD development and are unaware of risk factors that predict its development and future persistence. Therefore, young victims' psychological needs often remain unrecognized and unmet. Special attention should also be paid to the common occurrence of subsyndromal psychological disturbances and more complex syndromes (Schäfer et al. 2006).

More recently, Williams et al. (2015) reporting on a large representative sample of adolescents, as part of the 2005 National Survey of Adolescents-Replication (NSA-R) study, found that 10.2% of adolescents reported having at least 1 serious TA. The prevalence of current PTSD and depression among adolescents having a TA was 7.4% and 11.2%, respectively. A TA among thosed aged 15 years and younger was independently associated with depression and alcohol abuse while among adolescents aged 16 years and older, a TA was associated only with alcohol abuse.

While most studies agree on the high rates of PTSS/PTSD following TAs, Brand et al. (2014) found that the overall incidence of PTSD after TAs was very low (0.78% in a total of 32,807 collected data sets). The reason for this very low incidence of PTSD in their patient sample is attributed by the researchers to possible underestimation of the psychophysiological impact of traffic accidents on patients.

According to Meiser-Stedman et al. (2007), it is suggested that children should be directly interviewed as they are significantly more likely to meet criteria for ASD, as well as other ASD and PTSD symptom clusters, based on their own report than on their parent's report. Lastly, it is interesting to note that adolescent witnesses, as well as direct victims, may be at risk for posttraumatic reactions Tierens et al. (2012).

Risk Factors Related to Development of PTSS/PTSD

Certain factors have been found to predict development of PTSD/PTSS following TAs. One of them is gender: girls show greater risk for developing

PTSD than male victims of TAs (Kassam-Adams and Winston 2004, Mirza et al. 1998, Olofsson et al. 2008, Stallard et al. 2004). Acute stress disorder and general psychopathology such as anxiety and depression in young victims also predict the development of PTSS/PTSD (Bryant et al. 2004, Dalgleish et al. 2008, Mather et al. 2003, McDermott and Cvitanovich 2000, Mirza et al. 1998). Perceived threat has also been documented by some studies as being a predictor of PTSD (Bryant et al. 2004, Di Gallo et al. 1997, McDermott and Cvitanovich 2000, Stallard et al. 1998).

Age and socioeconomic status are not related to PTSD development among children and adolescents following TAs (Olofsson et al. 2009). Findings regarding type of TA and the severity of body injury as risk factors have been inconsistent (Keppel-Benson et al. 2002, Olofsson et al. 2009). However, the occurrence of brain injury after TAs has been correlated with PTSS, with mild brain injury predicting a higher risk of PTSD than no brain injury. Mather et al. (2003) have also found that the presence of mild TBI did not influence the likelihood of experiencing PTSS following a TA.

Maladaptive appraisals have been associated with the development and maintenance of pediatric PTSS/PTSD 6 months after TAs, whereas other cognitive processes, such as subjective threat and memory, may have a possible effect only in the acute phase (Meiser-Stedman et al. 2009). Stallard and Smith (2007) also found that the theoretically determined appraisals and cognitive coping styles of young victims of TAs were associated with chronic post-traumatic reactions; these authors also suggest the need to develop trauma-focused interventions for children that directly address these key cognitions during therapy.

Other predictors of PTSS among school-aged children include peri-traumatic distress, a robust predictor according to Bui et al. (2010) and posttraumatic nightmares--especially exact replicative ones (Wittmann et al. 2010).

Parental PTSS, depression, worry, vigilance, and general family functioning increase the risk of developing PTSD among children (De Vries et al. 1999, Keppel-Benson et al. 2002, Kolaitis et al. 2011, Landolt et al. 2005). This also suggests that parents should be actively involved in family prevention and treatment interventions of their children's PTSS/PTSD.

PTSD and Biological Markers

In one of the few existing studies, Kassam-Adams et al. (2005) have identified association between early physiological arousal (i.e., elevated heart rate defined as >/=2 SDs higher than the normal resting heart rate for their age and sex) and the development or persistence of PTSD symptoms in injured children and point to the importance of better understanding the interplay between physiological and psychological functioning after a traumatic stressor.

Neuroendocrine Perspectives of PTSD After TAs

During the last 30 years, a variety of published studies in trauma survivors have elucidated the role of the Hypothalamic-Pituitary-Adrenal (HPA) Axis and the Sympathetic Nervous System (SNS) in the pathophysiology of PTSD (Chrousos 2009, Pervanidou and Chrousos 2010). The HPA Axis and the SNS are the main components of the Stress System, via which the brain regulates the complex responses to threatening stimuli. The activation of the stress system by everyday stressors results in adaptive endocrine, metabolic, behavioral and cardiovascular changes that help maintain homeostasis. However, the experience of traumatic stressors, such as accidents, natural disasters, violent attacks, terrorism, or witnessing such exposures can lead to excessive and prolonged activation of stress mediators or, in a subgroup of individuals, to chronic hypoactivation of the stress system, which is equivalent to a state of dyshomeostasis with a variety of psychological and biological consequences (Pervanidou and Chrousos 2010, Chrousos 2009).

Summary of Studies in Adults with PTSD

The majority of studies in adults with PTSD have shown increased CRH centrally and decreased cortisol in the periphery, with elevated catecholamine concentrations. More specifically, the research has shown elevated basal cerebrospinal fluid (CSF) CRH levels, as indicated both by using a single lumbar puncture and serial CSF sampling (Bremner et al. 1997, Kasckow et al. 2001,) and low urinary cortisol concentrations (Yehuda et al. 1995, Yehuda 2001) and reduced blood cortisol concentrations, several times during the circadian cycle (Yehuda et al. 1993) or an altered circadian rhythm in salivary cortisol (Yehuda et al. 2005). Other studies have reported an increased number of lymphocyte glucocorticoid receptors (GRs) in patients with PTSD compared to controls (Yehuda et al. 1991). More recent studies show that salivary cortisol concentrations, as measured by single cortisol values, cortisol awakening response (CAR), area under the curve (AUC) and as responses to stress tests are all low in patients with PTSD (Wahbeh and Oken 2013).

Hair cortisol is a relatively new method, assessing cortisol exposure of tissues in the long-term. Recent evidence has shown that PTSD patients, as well as traumatized individuals without current PTSD, had decreased hair cortisol concentrations compared to controls, connecting trauma exposure per se with long-term basal cortisol concentrations (Steudte et al. 2013). In addition, the experience of multiple events, with a longer time since traumatization, were related to hypocortisolism (Steudte et al. 2013).

Catecholamine concentrations, have been determined in PTSD patients as biomarkers of SNS activity. Increased noradrenergic activity, both centrally (Geracioti et al. 2001) and peripherally, in 24h urine (Kasckow et al. 2001, Southwick et al. 1999) and in plasma seems to be the most consistent finding in PTSD patients. Mean plasma Norepinephrine (NE) and 3-methoxy-4-hydroxyphenylglycol, a metabolite of NE, concentrations were higher in war veterans with PTSD than in veterans with PTSD and co-morbid depression, patients with major depressive disorder (MDD) and healthy volunteers (Yehuda et al. 1998). Similarly, children with PTSD have increased peripheral sympathetic nervous system (SNS) activity (Delahanty et al. 2005, Pervanidou et al. 2007a). Furthermore, decreased platelet a2 receptor binding indicates NE hyperactivity in patients with PTSD (Vermetten and Bremner 2002, Strawn and Geracioti 2008).

In conclusion, the majority of studies reveal a unique pattern of stress system neuroendocrine function in individuals with PTSD, with paradoxically high CRH concentrations, centrally in the CSF and low cortisol peripherally in the systemic circulation, together with high central and peripheral catecholamines. Several pathophysiologic mechanisms have been proposed to elucidate the biological profile of PTSD: an increased cortisol signaling capacity may occur, so that lower cortisol concentrations may suppress more efficiently the HPA axis exerting increased negative feedback actions. This may lead to decreased exposure of the LC/SNS system to the negative actions of cortisol, contributing to increased sympathetic activation (Chrousos 2009, Pervanidou and Chrousos 2012).

Neuroendocrine Studies After TAs

Limited studies in adults and children have investigated stress hormones concentrations after accidents in relation to the development of PTSD: In a study of TA survivors attending an emergency department (Ehring et al. 2008) lower salivary cortisol concentrations after the accident predicted greater PTSD and depression levels 6 months after the event. In this study, low cortisol levels correlated with data-driven processing during the accident, and, in females, with prior trauma and prior emotional problems. Higher evening cortisol 6 months after the event correlated with PTSD and depressive symptoms at 6 months, but this relation was no longer significant when levels of pain were controlled. In a second study (Shalev et al. 2008) plasma and salivary cortisol, urinary excretion of cortisol, plasma levels of adrenocorticotropin (ACTH), and the leukocyte glucocorticoid receptor (GR) density were determined after the event in non-injured survivors of traumatic events, 125 of whom were involved in TAs, 19 in terrorist attacks and 11 in other events. Survivors with and without PTSD 5 months later, had similar levels of hormones at all times, whereas, plasma cortisol levels decreased with time in both groups. Female subjects had lower ACTH levels than males and PTSD in females was associated with higher levels of ACTH. In examining the adrenergic response in the same participants (Videlock et al. 2008), plasma levels and urinary excretion of norepinephrine (NE) were measured. Plasma NE levels were lower in subjects with PTSD at 10 days, 1 month, and 5 months after the event. The authors concluded that peripheral NE concentrations, shortly after traumatic events, are poor risk indicators of subsequent PTSD among civilian trauma victims.

The relations between urinary hormone levels collected upon admission to the trauma unit following a motor vehicle accident and PTSD symptomatology 1 month later was examined in a study of survivors of TAs (Delahanty et al. 2000). Participants subsequently diagnosed with acute PTSD excreted significantly lower levels of cortisol in 15-hour urines collected upon admission to the hospital. In addition, urinary levels of cortisol predicted a significant percentage of the variance in intrusive and avoidant thoughts 1 month after the accident.

Lastly, catecholamines were related to PTSD diagnosis and symptoms, only among men in a study of adults involved in serious TAs (Hawk et al. 2000) and in age-matched controls. PTSD-symptomatic men exhibited elevated epinephrine and norepinephrine concentrations 1 month after the TA and had higher epinephrine levels 5 months later. Urinary cortisol was also elevated among PTSD-symptomatic men, but not women, and only immediately (1 month) after the accident. For men and women, greater emotional numbing predicted a lower cortisol level 6 months after the accident.

Neuroendocrine Studies in Children

Although the majority of studies in adults with PTSD show low peripheral cortisol concentrations as a biomarker of HPA axis function, diverse patterns of aberrant cortisol secretion have been reported in this disorder in children. However, markers of SNS activity are more consistent between patients, mostly showing high plasma and/or urine catecholamine concentrations.

Several parameters affect the direction of the HPA axis (increased or decreased cortisol production) in PTSD, and among them, the nature of the trauma (single acute or chronic), previous trauma and time since the trauma occurred seem to be crucial determinants of hyper- or hypo- activation of the HPA axis.

Scarce data exist on the longitudinal course of PTSD development and maintenance, beginning from the exposure to a single, acute traumatic event.

After a TA, initial 12-h urinary cortisol concentrations in children involved in such accidents, significantly correlated with subsequent acute PTSD symptoms (Delahanty et al. 2005). After removing the variance associated with demographic variables and depressive symptoms, urinary cortisol and epinephrine levels continued to predict a significant percentage (7-10%) of the variance in 6-week PTSD symptoms. Separate gender analysis suggested that significance was primarily driven by the relations between hormone levels and acute PTSD symptoms in boys.

In an earlier work, we investigated the natural history of neuroendocrine changes in relation to PTSD development in children and adolescents experiencing a TA (Pervanidou et al. 2007a,b). The participants had no history of previous traumatic exposures, nor current or lifetime psychopathology. We compared salivary cortisol, plasma catecholamines and serum interleukin (IL)-6 among children that developed PTSD one month after the accident (30%), with a group that experienced the traumatic event but did not develop PTSD and a control group. In addition, we compared the above mentioned biomarkers among the sub-group (15%) that developed at month one but also maintained PTSD diagnosis six months after the accident, with those free of PTSD at both months one and six and the control group.

Evening (9.00 p.m.) salivary cortisol and morning (8.00 a.m.) serum IL-6, within 24 hours after the event, were highly inter-related and both predictive of PTSD development at month 6 (Pervanidou 2008). The PTSD group exhibited higher NE concentrations compared to the other two groups at both assessments. Interestingly, NE concentrations became gradually greater within the longitudinal PTSD group, from month 1 to month 6. In children with PTSD, as evening cortisol concentrations and circadian rhythm normalized at month 6, NE elevations became greater (Pervanidou et al. 2007a).

This longitudinal study provided evidence for an initial elevation of cortisol and an alteration in cortisol circadian secretion in response to the experience of an intense stressor. This initial alteration is followed by a gradual normalization of cortisol with time, leading potentially to decreased cortisol concentrations in the periphery, months or years after the traumatic exposure. At the same time, a progressive elevation of circulating NE was noted in children that continued to exhibit PTSD. This longitudinal interaction of peripheral cortisol and noradrenaline concentrations seems to characterize those that develop and maintain PTSD. Thus, low cortisol, together with high NE concentrations, that characterize adult PTSD, may be the end stage of the disorder (Pervanidou et al. 2008). These data are also in accordance with findings in adults, showing hypocortisolism in the aftermath of a stressful experience to predict PTSD development. In those individuals exhibiting low cortisol concentrations after the experience of an acute stressor, hypocortisolism might reflect previous traumatization, and, thus represents a biological vulnerability factor for further PTSD development (Pervanidou et al. 2008).

Traffic Accidents and Health-Related Quality of Life

There are not many studies in the literature on TAs and impact on young victims' HRQoL. Short-term adverse changes in the child's HRQoL were observed for the child's motor functioning and autonomy by Sturms et al. (2005). A prospective study (Landolt et al. 2009) gave evidence for a long-term negative influence of early PTSS on HRQoL in injured children. The return of injured children to pre-injury HRQoL may therefore not only depend on optimal medical care but also on awareness and timely interventions regarding PTSS.

COPING

In their study, Stallard et al. (2001) found that children involved in TAs used between 5 and 7 different coping strategies. Younger children and those with PTSD used more strategies than older children and those not suffering from PTSD. Children with PTSD were more likely to use the strategies of distraction, social withdrawal, emotional regulation and blaming others. Stallard and Smith (2007) gave support to the applicability of the Ehlers and Clark (2000) cognitive model to children. Their results indicate that the theoretically determined appraisals and cognitive coping styles are associated with chronic post-traumatic reactions. Also, their findings suggest the need to develop trauma-focused interventions for children that directly address these key cognitions during therapy. In another study, Keppel-Benson et al. (2002) suggest the possible inoculating role of previous accidents and the importance of social support following TAs.

CONCLUSION

Traffic accidents are a major cause for injury in children and adolescents. Even after 'everyday' TAs, psychological consequences are common in many victims, such as PTSD, traffic-related fears or mood disturbances. Any child will be at risk of PTSD/PTSS, not just those with severe injuries. Almost one third of children injured in TAs will develop PTSD/PTSS in the first month and half of them after 3-6 months, or the initially developed PTSD will decrease to the same level as PTSS at 3-6 months. High levels of distress during and immediately after the accident are associated with severe PTSS. Therefore, routine evaluation of the psychological impact of TAs should receive the same priority as screening for physical injury. Liaison with accident and emergency departments would enhance the early detection and follow-up of children at risk of developing PTSD. Young victims of TAs should be directly interviewed particularly for the early screening of posttraumatic stress. The possibility of delayed onset of PTSS implies a monitoring beyond the first weeks after the accident. Active management and referral for treatment as well as identification of children at risk and prevention of PTSD and other psychosocial consequences are important. More studies on the mechanisms underlying the development of PTSS/PTSD and also studies on the psychobiology of physical trauma and PTSD in this pediatric population are needed. A major role of public health should be in the prevention of TAs, especially in low- and middle-income countries, and their consequences.

References

Bremner JD, Licinio J, Dammel A, Krystal JH, Owens MJ, Southwick SM, Nemeroff CB, Charney DS (1997). Elevated CSF corticotropin-releasing factor concentrations in posttraumatic stress disorder. *Am J Psychiatry,* 154, 624–629.

Bryant B, Mayou R, Wiggs L, Ehlers A, Stores G. (2004). Psychological consequences of road traffic accidents for children and their mothers. *Psychol Med,* 34(2), 335-46.

Bui E, Brunet A, Allenou C, Camassel C, Raynaud JP, Claudet I, Fries F, Cahuzac JP, Grandjean H, Schmitt L, Birmes P (2010). Peritraumatic reactions and posttraumatic stress symptoms in school-aged children victims of road traffic accident. Gen Hosp Psychiatry, 32(3), 330-3. doi: 10.1016/j.genhosppsych.2010.01.014. Epub 2010 Mar 1.

Chrousos GP (2009) Stress and disorders of the stress system. *Nat Rev Endocrinology,* 5(7), 374-81.

Commission for Global Road Safety. (2006). Make Roads Safe. A New Priority for Sustainable Development, Commission for Global Road Safety, London.

Dalgleish T, Meiser-Stedman R, Kassam-Adams N, Ehlers A, Winston F, Smith P, Bryant B, Mayou RA, Yule W (2008). Predictive validity of acute stress disorder in children and adolescents. *Br J Psychiatry,* 5, 392-3. doi: 10.1192/bjp.bp.107.040451.

Delahanty DL, Nugent N R, Christopher N C, and Walsh M (2005). Initial urinary epinephrine and cortisol levels predict acute PTSD symptoms in child trauma victims. *Psychoneuroendocrinology,* 30 (2), 121–128.

Delahanty DL, Raimonde AJ, Spoonster E (2000). Initial posttraumatic urinary cortisol levels predict subsequent PTSD symptoms in motor vehicle accident victims. *Biol Psychiatry,* 48(9), 940-7.

de Vries AP, Kassam-Adams N, Cnaan A, Sherman-Slate E, Gallagher PR, Winston FK (1999). Looking beyond the physical injury: posttraumatic stress disorder in children and parents after pediatric traffic injury. *Pediatrics.* 104(6), 1293-9.

Di Gallo A, Barton J, Parry-Jones WL (1997). Road traffic accidents: early psychological consequences in children and adolescents. *Br J Psychiatry,* 170, 358-62.

Ehlers A, Clark DM (2000). A cognitive model of posttraumatic stress disorder. Behav Res Ther, 38(4), 319-45. Review.

Ehring T, Ehlers A, Cleare AJ, Glucksman E (2008). Do acute psychological and psychobiological responses to trauma predict subsequent symptom severities of PTSD and depression? *Psychiatry Res,* 161(1), 67-75.

Geracioti TD Jr, Baker DG, Ekhator NN, West SA, Hill KK, Bruce AB, Schmidt D, Rounds-Kugler B, Yehuda R, Keck PE Jr, Kasckow JW (2001). CSF norepinephrine concentrations in posttraumatic stress disorder. *Am J Psychiatry,* 158(8), 1227-30.

Hawk LW(1), Dougall AL, Ursano RJ, Baum A (2000). Urinary catecholamines and cortisol in recent-onset posttraumatic stress disorder after motor vehicle accidents. *Psychosom Med,* 62(3), 423-34.

Kasckow JW, Baker D, Geracioti TD Jr (2001). Corticotropin-releasing hormone in depression and post-traumatic stress disorder. *Peptides,* 22(5), 845-851.

Kassam-Adams N, Garcia-España JF, Fein JA, Winston FK (2005). Heart rate and posttraumatic stress in injured children. *Arch Gen Psychiatry,* 62(3), 335-40.

Keppel-Benson JM, Ollendick TH, Benson MJ (2002). Post-traumatic stress in children following motor vehicle accidents. *J Child Psychol Psychiatry.* 43(2), 203-12.

Kolaitis, G., Giannakopoulos, G., Liakopoulou, M., Pervanidou, P., Charitaki, S., Mihas, C., Ferentinos, S., Papassotiriou, I., Chrousos, G.P., Tsiantis, J. (2011). Predicting pediatric posttraumatic stress disorder after road traffic accidents: the role of parental psychopathology. *J Trauma Stress* 24, 414-421.

Landolt MA, Vollrath ME, Gnehm HE, Sennhauser FH (2009). Post-traumatic stress impacts on quality of life in children after road traffic accidents: prospective study. *Aust N Z J Psychiatry,* 43(8), 746-53. doi: 10.1080/00048670903001919.

Landolt MA, Vollrath M, Timm K, Gnehm HE, Sennhauser FH (2005). Predicting posttraumatic stress symptoms in children after road traffic accidents. *J Am Acad Child Adolesc Psychiatry,* 44(12), 1276-83.

Mather FJ, Tate RL, Hannan TJ (2003). Post-traumatic stress disorder in children following road traffic accidents: a comparison of those with and without mild traumatic brain injury. *Brain Inj,* 17(12), 1077-87.

McDermott BM, Cvitanovich A (2000). Posttraumatic stress disorder and emotional problems in children following motor vehicle accidents: an extended case series. *Aust N Z J Psychiatry,* 34(3), 446-52.

Mehta S, Ameratunga SN (2012). Prevalence of post-traumatic stress disorder among children and adolescents who survive road traffic crashes: a systematic review of the international literature. *J Paediatr Child Health,* 48(10), 876-85. doi: 10.1111/j.1440-1754.2011.02076.x. Epub 2011 Apr 29.

Meiser-Stedman R, Dalgleish T, Glucksman E, Yule W, Smith P (2009). Maladaptive cognitive appraisals mediate the evolution of posttraumatic stress reactions: A 6-month follow-up of child and adolescent assault and motor vehicle accident survivors. *J Abnorm Psychol,*18(4), 778-87. doi: 10.1037/a0016945.

Meiser-Stedman R, Smith P, Glucksman E, Yule W, Dalgleish T (2007). Parent and child agreement for acute stress disorder, post-traumatic stress disorder and other psychopathology in a prospective study of children and adolescents exposed to single-event trauma. *J Abnorm Child Psychol.* Apr;35(2):191-201.

Meiser-Stedman R, Yule W, Smith P, Glucksman E, Dalgleish T (2005). Acute stress disorder and posttraumatic stress disorder in children and adolescents involved in assaults or motor vehicle accidents. *Am J Psychiatry,* 162(7), 1381-3.

Mirza KA, Bhadrinath BR, Goodyer IM, Gilmour C (1998). Post-traumatic stress disorder in children and adolescents following road traffic accidents. *Br J Psychiatry,* 172, 443-7.

Olofsson E, Bunketorp O, Andersson AL (2009). Children and adolescents injured in traffic--associated psychological consequences: a literature review. J Trauma Stress 25(3), 280-7. doi: 10.1002/jts.21692. Epub 2012 Jun 8.

Peden M, Scurfield R, Sleet D, Mohan D, Hyder AA, Jarawan E and Mathers C (Eds). World report on road traffic injury prevention. Geneva: World Health Organization, 2004.

Pervanidou P, Kolaitis G, Charitaki S, Lazaropoulou Ch, Papassotiriou I, Hindmarsh P, Bakoula Ch, Tsiantis J and Chrousos GP (2007a). The Natural History of Neuroendocrine Changes in Pediatric Post-traumatic Stress Disorder (PTSD) after Motor Vehicle Accidents: Progressive Divergence of Noradrenaline and Cortisol Concentrations over Time. *Biol Psychiatry,* 62 (10): 1095-1102.

Pervanidou P, Kolaitis G, Charitaki S, Bakoula Ch, Margeli A, Lazaropoulou Ch, Papassotiriou I, Tsiantis J and Chrousos GP (2007b). Elevated Salivary Cortisol and Serum Interleukin (IL)-6 Concentrations after Motor Vehicle Accidents may predict Posttraumatic Stress Disorder in Children and Adolescents. *Psychoneuroendocrinology,* 32 (8-10), 991-999.

Pervanidou P (2008). Biology of Posttraumatic Stress Disorder in childhood and adolescence. *J Neuroendocrinology,* 20(5), 632–638.

Pervanidou, P, Chrousos, GP (2010) Neuroendocrinology of post-traumatic stress disorder. *Prog Brain Res.;*182:149-60.

Pervanidou P, Chrousos GP (2012). Posttraumatic stress disorder in children and adolescents: neuroendocrine perspectives. *Sci Signal,* 5(245), pt6

Schäfer I, Barkmann C, Riedesser P, Schulte-Markwort M (2006). Posttraumatic syndromes in children and adolescents after road traffic accidents--a prospective cohort study. *Psychopathology,* 39(4), 159-64. Epub 2006 Apr 11.

Shalev AY, Videlock EJ, Peleg T, Segman R, Pitman RK, Yehuda R. (2008). Stress hormones and post-traumatic stress disorder in civilian trauma victims: a longitudinal study. Part I: HPA axis responses. *Int J Neuropsychopharmacol,* 11(3), 365-72.

Southwick SM, Paige S, Morgan CA, Bremmer JD, Krystal JH, and Charney DS. (1999). Neurotransmitter alterations in PTSD: Catecholamines and serotonin. *Sem Clin Neuropsychiatry,* 4(4), 242–248.

Stallard P, Velleman R, Baldwin S (1998). Prospective study of post-traumatic stress disorder in children involved in road traffic accidents. *BMJ,* 12, 317(7173), 1619-23.

Stallard P, Velleman R, Langsford J, Baldwin S. (2001). Coping and psychological distress in children involved in road traffic accidents. *Br J Clin Psychol,* 40(Pt 2), 197-208.

Stallard P, Smith E (2007). Appraisals and cognitive coping styles associated with chronic post-traumatic symptoms in child road traffic accident survivors. *J Child Psychol Psychiatry,* 48(2), 194-201.

Stallard P, Salter E, Velleman R. (2004). Posttraumatic stress disorder following road traffic accidents - a second prospective study. *Eur Child Adolesc Psychiatry,* 13(3), 172-8.

Steudte S, Kirschbaum C, Gao W, Alexander N, Schönfeld S, Hoyer J, Stalder T (2013). Hair cortisol as a biomarker of traumatization in healthy individuals and posttraumatic stress disorder patients. *Biol Psychiatry,* 74(9), 639-646.

indicator of the severity of the accidents and can be used to monitor trends and to quantify the event that represents a cost to health services, due to the high percentage of hospital admissions and high hospital care costs.

Strategies should be implemented to propose prevention and control of traffic accidents, also specifically directed to motorcyclists.

1. Introduction

Traffic accidents represent a significant public health issue and are associated with behavioral factors, vehicles safeties and conditions of the urban spaces [1]. It appears as an important cause of morbidity and mortality due to the increasing number of automotive vehicles fleet, with the motorcycle among them [1, 2].

In the past few years, there has been an increasing number of motorcycle accidents, a vehicle which has been gaining acceptance and approval of the population for being agile, economical and with a reduced cost [3, 4].

According to Sant`Anna and cols [5] the popularization of this vehicle (motorcycle) is justified by its traffic flow capacity, fuel economy, parking facility, expansion in the market delivery and moto taxi, as well as the credit facilities for its acquisition in recent years [5]. Would this be an international reality? Or just in Latin America?

For the motorcyclist group, despite all the advances made by modern vehicle designs and safety devices, the inequalities in protective conditions or of its higher exposure on the roads, compared to users of other vehicles, it's the determining factor of higher morbidity and mortality [6, 7].

Injuries derived from traumatic events caused by motorcycle accidents, often result in temporary or permanent disabilities, which affects the life quality of the victims, and may even progress to death [8, 9].

Therefore, these accidents determine a lot of damages to the victim and to the society, such as high medical and hospital costs; absence from work; expenses with compensation; among others.

The knowledge of the risk factors related to morbidity and mortality of victims from motorcycle accidents, facilitate the understanding of the reality of these events. It helps to improve the planning, specific decision making and provides information about the characteristics of these occurrences [6].

The health sector bears the greatest burden of all consequences from the accidents, it is the one who provides the care of victims, counts deaths and assumes the aspects related to the after effects, which are quite often irreversible.

The implications of accidents involving motorcyclists demand for a pre-hospital, a hospital and rehabilitation care. As well as the disabilities generated, the potential years of life lost, the impact on the victim's families and society in general, have led institutions around the world to recognize the burden that these events produce on health systems and the significant social and economic costs they represent [10].

1.1. Factors Related to Motorcycle Accidents

The motorcycle became the most commonly used vehicle by the young population, especially males. Whether used as transportation, entertainment, sport or even as a working instrument [11, 12].

There are some given suggestions, for solving the problem of road traffic accidents involving a motorcyclist, which goes through quality and preventive vehicle maintenance, roads conditions, use of personal protective equipment and user's safe behavior [11].

One of the factors to be pointed out is the economic growth, associated with the increase of transport infrastructures, in which the population mobility becomes a key factor for their need and satisfaction. The increased demand and utilization of motorcycles require a proper urban infrastructure since the motorcycles are competing space with cars, further exacerbating the risks of injury and death among motorcyclists [12].

It is important to point out that there is a need for traffic education, lighting quality and signaling pathways. The planning for preventive measures should include the level of illumination on the roads and proper signaling as a safety parameter. These would be alternatives to prevent accidents between cars and motorcycles.

The occurrence of accidents may be related to the weekday and period. Some studies, suggest a higher incidence in the evenings and weekends, and a few factors pointed out as a risky behavior in traffic are: driving after drinking alcohol or using drugs, adopting rates above the road limit, driving on the side of the road, participation in car races, no overtaking and overpass a red traffic light [13, 14].

Some studies have indicated that one of the risk factors for victims of motorcycle accidents are not having license to drive, individuals with shorter qualification [15, 16, 17].

Greater the involvement of young male motorcycle riders on weekends, described in the literature, suggests a link between the accidents and the use of psychoactive substances, such as alcohol and illicit drugs [18, 19].

Regarding the increase of motorcycle accidents and its occurrence on the weekends, certain unanimity is registered among researchers. They relate this fact to the possible alcohol ingestion, more frequent during these periods [18, 19, 20].

The behavior of drinking alcohol and driving, the characteristics of drivers and the risk of accidents, is the object of study in research in several countries.

The relevance of drinking and driving to the public health caused many countries to adopt successfully, measures to reduce morbidity and mortality in traffic [21].

The consequences of the accidents to the health care system and society, point out the need for further information improvement from these causes, in order to support public policies for the prevention of injuries, comprehensive care for victims and health promotion [22].

1.2. Injuries Caused by Motorcycle Accidents

The morbidity and mortality due to traffic accidents, is extremely high around the world. However, the proportion of deaths and injuries from motorcycle accidents is particularly high, often a result of higher exposure, a disregard of traffic laws and adoption of risk behaviors [6].

The study of lesion patterns in traffic accident victims, seek to describe the types, locations and different types of trauma [9].

The body regions most affected have been described in several studies, which indicated lesions most often on lower limbs, followed by injuries in the upper limbs and injuries on the external surface [6, 9, 23].

The occurrence of lesions in the lower pelvis and members of the victims from motorcycle accidents, have been related to the fact that in frontal collisions suffered by victims, the bike leans forward throwing the motorcyclist against the handlebars, and if the legs and feet remain fixed on the pedals, the thigh is thrown against the handlebars and may cause bilateral lesions on the limbs. When there is a lateral collision, injuries happen because of the pressure against the bulkhead or because of another vehicle involved in the accident [23].

The limbs are noted as the regions most frequently injured in a motorcycle accident being the head less frequently compromised [24].

For motorcyclists, limbs are precisely the most vulnerable regions, since the use of safety equipment protects only the region of the head. There are some literature reports, who claimed that the actual helmet use reduced significantly the severity of head and neck injuries, but had no effect on overall severity of the lesions in other parts of the body [24].

For the motorcycle driver, exposure to trauma and consistent absorption of kinetic energy on their entire body surface, makes them extremely vulnerable to this type of accident, which usually has a multifactorial origin, including: the motorcycle storage conditions; the conservation state of public roads; safety signaling; the speed of the vehicles involved; visibility; traffic conditions; rain influence; respect for the legislation and inspection and human factor [25].

Injuries such as: excoriation, cuts, concussion, open and close fractures are directly related to the biomechanics of motorcycle accident, which is characterized by the power of the impact, absorbed by the body surface of the victim and often throwing them to the ground. The projected victims suffer, not only the crash impact, but also the collision against the ground, often followed by slippage, which increases the likelihood of severe injuries and the need for hospitalization [25, 26].

It's worth mentioning that superficial wounds such as abrasions and concussion, may be associated with deep tissue damages, and undetected at the time of the accident, requiring a more detailed diagnostic approach. In addition, injuries by skin breakdown, as occurs in the case of excoriation, cuts and blunt injuries may pose a risk of bleeding and infection [25].

Regarding exposed fractures, it increases the risk of osteomyelitis, sepsis and bone necrosis, in addition, exposed tendons become necrotic and dried, and exposed blood vessels are at risk of rupture, increasing the severity of the accident [25].

In cases of concussion on the chest and abdomen, it may cause injuries on the lungs, heart and abdominal organs, leading to internal bleedings, and consequently causing shock and death [25].

The inadequacy of some protective equipment and the indifference of drivers with its use, are associated with a high injury rate.

1.3. Motorcycle Accidents and Victims of Collision

Pedestrian collisions result from various factors. Many of them are related to the local conditions, others to personal conduct. The signaling conditions at the scene are directly related to pedestrian trauma [27, 28].

Pedestrians and motorcyclists are the predominate victims of road accidents. It is inferred that the highest mortality in the pedestrian group injuries from a traffic accident caused by motorcycle is due to higher body exposure, with no protective devices to minimize damages at the time of the accident [29].

The way of driving and the vulnerability of the driver contributed to the increase in accidents involving motorcyclists, and its main victims, the pedestrians. According to Bacchieri and Barros in 2011, the motorcycle drivers are considered the priority group for prevention programs, with risks seven times higher of death, four times of physical injury and twice running over a pedestrian, when compared to car drivers [30].

Pedestrians are the most vulnerable users on the road system, they make up the largest percentage of victims, in addition to this they are faced with narrow sidewalks and sometimes without proper conservation [31].

Children and seniors, represent an important portion of victims of pedestrian accidents. Studies conducted by Katz et al. (2008), verified that the most prevalent mechanism of trauma in the elderly is trampling, mainly resulting in fractures of lower limbs [32].

The number of pedestrian accidents is considered high in the population with age under 20 and over 70 years old, the latter ones being the main victims, due to their own physical changes of aging (more restricted mobility, lack of attention, visual and hearing difficulties, and others), and also as a result of the intransigence of our drivers [33].

Regarding the pedestrian accidents, including children and adolescents, a study conducted by Waksman (2005) verified that these accidents may be linked to the lack of knowledge and maturity to cross the streets [34].

Researches about pedestrian accidents are important to build up a reliable local knowledge and to guide effective interventions.

1.4. Prevention of Accidents

Traffic accidents, including the ones involving motorcycles, are among the leading causes of death and disability worldwide, and is projected to be responsible for increasing more and more the public health costs [35].

Over speeding in traffic is a serious safety problem in many countries, contributing in part to traffic injuries, and in additional for being an aggravating factor in these events. The higher the speed, designed by the vehicle, higher is the risk of collision and probability of serious injuries [35].

Interventions designed to reduce traffic speed, are considered essential for preventing traffic accidents. Among these, we can mention the implementation of speed control radars [35]. One of the effects from the application of electronic speed detectors, quoted by Oliveira and cols [35], is the tendency of some drivers to stop when passing through radar, and then to exceed the speed limit, when out of reach. New strategies are needed, to mitigate against this effect, combined with cultural changes in over speeding practice, in order to have a positive effect on the behavior of drivers, in relation to the radars. A relatively new method, who has the potential to restrain the mentioned effect, is the path control or average speed check. In contrast, to the conventional automatic speed systems, measuring the speed of a vehicle at one point, the ride control system, measures the average speed, over a distance of at least 500 meters to several kilometers [35].

Regarding road safeties, there are listed as priority some risk factors for traffic accidents, involving motorcycles, such as: speed, alcohol abuse, as well as the non-use of helmets and protective clothing [36].

Regarding the suspicion of alcohol ingestion, studies indicate a strong correlation between alcohol ingestion, and traffic accidents, since the beverage generates a sense of confidence in conductors, while it decreases their reaction and time coordination skills [36, 37]. Personal beliefs, related to their health maintenance, are an important factor in determining health behaviors. Among these of importance in preventing traffic accidents, we can mention the habit of not drinking alcohol while driving. Beliefs regarding the importance of healthy habits, influence not only behaviors, but also attitudes towards legislation, such as self-care with the use of specific protections, social policy decisions, and healthy lifestyle promotional programs [38].

The regulation of laws that requires the use of protections, for the upper and lower limbs, and health promotion actions, appears as suggestions for the prevention of traffic accidents involving motorcyclists [39].

Although the act of sleeping is an important cause of accidents, it is very little studied, especially due to the difficulty of investigating this variable, after the occurrence of an accident [39]. Sleepiness, is often ignored because of the lack recognition of drivers, who attributes the accident to other causes, such as bad weather conditions, or insufficient state of preservation of the freeway [39].

Another worrying factor is related, to the use of illicit and psychoactive drugs, but studies about the influence of these substances, becomes impractical due to the difficulty of showing their presence [40, 41]. It is necessary real education, about the risks of driving under influence, and higher surveillance on highways, and urban centers.

Conclusion

Traffic accidents with motorcyclists, are in large part predictable, and can be prevented. It is therefore, an issue susceptible to rational analysis, and intervention. The health situation analysis can help in the action planning and facing the issue. Preventing accidents is a matter of Public Health, whose actions should include intersectional coordination. Studies on this topic, improvements, integration of databases, and evaluation of interventions, are some initiatives to be encouraged.

References

[1] Paixão L. M. M. M., Contijo E. D., Mingoti A. S., Costa D. A. S., Friche A. A. L., Caiaffa W. T. Urban road traffic deaths: data linkage and identification of high-risk population sub-groups. *Cad. Saude Publica*. 2015; 31 (supl. 1): 92-106.

[2] Oliveira A. L., Petroianu A., Gonçalves D. M. V., Pereira G. A., Alberti L. R. Characteristics of motorcyclists involved in accidents between motorcycles and automobiles. *Rev. Assoc. Med. Bras*. 2015; 61 (1): 61-64.

[3] Rodrigues C. L., Armond J. E., Gorios C., Souza P. C. Accidents involving motorcyclists and cyclists in the municipality of São Paulo: characterization and trends. *Rev. Bras. Ortop*. 2014; 49 (6): 602-606.

[4] Gorios C., Armond J. E., Rodrigues C. L., Pernambuco H., Iporre R. O., Souza P. C. Analysis of hospitalization occurred due to motorcycles accidents in São Paulo city. *Acta Ortop Bras*. 2015; 23 (4): 212-214.

[5] Sant'Anna F. L., Andrade S. M., Sant'Anna F. H. M., Liberatti C. L. B. Acidentes com motociclistas: comparação entre os anos 1998 e 2010. Londrina, PR, Brasil. *Rev. Saúde Pública*. 2013; 47 (3): 607-615.

[6] Oliveira N. L. B., Sousa R. M. C. Risco de lesões em motociclistas nas ocorrências de trânsito. *Rev. Esc. Enferm. USP*. 2012; 46 (5): 1133-1140.

[7] Day L., Lenné M. G., Symmons M., Hillard P., Newstead S., Allen T., McClure R. Population based case-control study of serious non-fatal motorcycle crashes. *BMC Public Health*. 2013; 13 (72): 1-6.

[8] Le L. C., Blum R. W. Road traffic injury among young people in Vietnam: evidence from two rounds of national adolescent health surveys, 2004-2009. *Glob. Health Action*. 2013; 6: 1-9.

[9] Debieux P., Chertaman C., Mansur N. S. B., Dobashi E., Fernandes H. J. A. Musculoskeletal injuries in motorcycle accidents. *Acta Ortop Bras*. 2010; 18 (6): 353-356.

[10] Cabral A. P. S., Souza W. V., Lima L. M. C. Serviço de Atendimento Móvel de Urgência: Um observatório dos acidentes de transportes terrestre em nível local. *Rev. bras. epidemiol*. 2011; 14 (1): 3-14.

[11] Pordeus A. M. J., Vieira L. J. E. S., Almeida P. C., Andrade L. M., Silva A. C. G., Lira S. V. G. Fatores associados à ocorrência do acidente de motocicleta na percepção do motociclista hospitalizado. *Rev. bras. promoç. saúde*. 2010; 23 (3): 206-212.

[12] Rodrigues E. M. S., Villaveces V., Sanhueza A., Escamilla-Cejudo J. A. Trends in fatal motorcycle injuries in the Americas, 1998-2010. *International Journal of Injury Control and Safety Promotion*. 2014; 21 (2): 170-180.

[13] Golias A. R. C., Caetano R. Acidentes entre motocicletas: análise dos casos ocorridos no estado do Paraná entre julho de 2010 e junho de 2011. *Ciênc. Saúde coletiva*. 2013; 18 (5): 1235-1246.

[14] Perez-Fuster P., Rodrigo M. F., Ballestar M. L., Sanmartin J. Modeling offenses among motorcyclists involved in crashes in Spain. *Accid Anal Prev*. 2013; 56: 95-102.

[15] Soares L. S., Sousa D. A. C. M., Machado A. L. G., Silva G. R. F. Caracterização das vítimas de traumas por acidente com motocicleta internadas em um hospital público. *Rev enferm UERJ*. 2015; 23 (1):115-121.

[16] Zabeu J. L. A., Zovico J. R. R., Pereira Júnior W. N., Tucci Neto P. F. Profile of motorcycle victims from the emergency service of a University Hospital. *Rev Bras Ortop*. 2013; 48 (3): 242-245.

[17] Yeh T.-H., Chang H.-L., Chang H.-W. Initial age of unlicensed motorcycling experience for a cohort of high school students. *Accid Anal Prev*. 2008; 40 (2): 511-517.

[18] Paixão L. M. M., Contijo E. D., Drumond E. F., Friche A. A. L., Caiaffa W. T. Acidentes de trânsito em Belo Horizonte: o que revelam três diferentes fontes de informações, 2008 a 2010. *Rev. bras. epidemiol.* 2015; 18 (1): 108-122.

[19] Baldock M. R., Lindsay V. L. Examination of the role of the combination of alcohol and cannabis in South Australian road crashes. *Traffic Inj Prev*. 2015; 16 (5): 443-449.

[20] Santos A. M. R., Moura M. E. B., Nunes B. M. V. T., Leal C. F. S., Teles J. B. M. Perfil das vítimas de trauma por acidente de moto atendidas em um serviço público de emergência. *Cad. Saúde Pública*. 2008; 24 (8): 1927-1938.

[21] Campos V. R., Salgado R. S., Rocha M. C. Bafômetro positivo: correlatos do comportamento de beber e dirigir na cidade de Belo Horizonte, Minas Gerais, Brasil. *Cad. Saúde Pública*. 2013; 29 (1): 51-61.

[22] Brasil. Ministério da Saúde. *Viva: vigilância de violências e acidentes, 2006 e 2007*; Brasília: 2009.

[23] Pinto A. O., Witt R. R. Gravidade de lesões e características de motociclistas atendidos em um hospital de pronto socorro. o. *Rev Gaúcha Enferm*. 2008; 29 (3):408-414.

[24] Oliveira N. L. B., Souza R. M. C. Diagnóstico de lesões e qualidade de vida de motociclistas, vítimas de acidentes de trânsito. *Rev. Latino-Am. Enfermagem*. 2003; 11 (6): 749-756.

[25] Tavares F. L., Leite F. M. C., Lima E. F. A., Cade N. V., Coelho M. J. Homens e acidentes motociclísticos: gravidade dos acidentados a partir do atendimento pré-hospitalar. *J. res.: fundam. care. online* 2016; 8 (1): 4004-4014.

[26] Rezende Neta D. S., Alves A. K., Leão G. M., Araújo A. A. Perfil das ocorrências de politrauma em condutores motociclísticos atendidos pelo SAMU de Teresina-PI. *Rev. bras. enferm.* 2012; 65 (6): 936-941.

[27] Parreira J. G., Martins R. K., Slongo J., Perlingeiro J. A. G., Soldá S. C., Assef J. C. Análise comparativa das lesões diagnosticadas e de sua

gravidade entre vítimas de atropelamento e outros mecanismos de trauma fechado. *Rev. Col. Bras. Cir.* 2015; 42 (4): 253-258.

[28] Herrero-Hernandez, D. Desarrollo de un cuestionario breve para la medición del comportamiento arriesgado en peatones adolescentes. *Rev. colomb. Psicol.*. 2015; 24(2): 271-284.

[29] Papa M. A. F., Wisnieswski D., Inoue K. C., Molena-Fernandes A., Évora I. D. M., Matsuda L. M. Mortality from land transport accidents: A comparative analysis. *Cogitare Enferm.* 2014; 19 (1):47-54.

[30] Bacchieri G., Barros A. J. D. Traffi c accidents in Brazil from 1998 to 2010: many changes and few effects. *Rev Saude Publica.* 2011; 45 (5): 949-963.

[31] Almeida R. L. F., Bezerra Filho J. G., Braga J. U., Magalhães F. B., Macedo M. C. M., Silva K. A. Via, homem e veículo: fatores de risco associados à gravidade dos acidentes de trânsito. *Rev. Saúde Pública.* 2013; 47 (4): 718-731.

[32] Katz M., Okuma M. A. A., Santos A. L. G., Guglielmetti C. L. B., Sakaki M. H., Zumiotti A. V. Epidemiologia das lesões traumáticas de alta energia em idosos. *Acta ortop. bras.* 2008; 16 (5): 279-283.

[33] Silveira R., Rodrigues R. A. P., Costa Junior M. L. Idosos que foram vítimas de acidentes de trânsito no município de Ribeirão Preto-SP, em 1998. *Rev. Latino-Am. Enfermagem.* 2002; 10 (6): 765-771.

[34] Waksman R. D., Pirito R. M. B. K. O pediatra e a segurança no trânsito. *J. Pediatr.* 2005; 81 [supl. 5]: 181-188.

[35] Oliveira D. F., Friche A. A. L., Costa D. A. S., Mingoti A. S., Caiaffa W. T. Do speed cameras reduce speeding in urban areas? *Cad. Saúde Pública.* 2015; 31 [Sup]: S1-S12.

[36] Fantoni R., Volpe F. M. A subjetividade na avaliação do risco e sua influência nas políticas públicas de prevenção da violência no trânsito. *Rev Med Minas Gerais* 2014; 24 [Supl 5]: S47-S56.

[37] Tavares F. L., Coelho M. J., Leite F. M. C. Men and motorcycles accidents: characterization of accidents from pre hospital care. *Esc Anna Nery.* 2014; 18 (4): 656-661.

[38] Marín L., Queiroz M. S. A atualidade dos acidentes de trânsito na era da velocidade: uma visão geral. *Cad. Saúde Pública.* 2000; 16 (1): 7-21.

[39] Veronese A. M., Oliveira D. L. L. C. Os riscos dos acidentes de trânsito na perspectiva dos moto-boys: subsídios para a promoção da saúde. *Cad. Saúde Pública.* 2006; 22 (12): 2717-2721.

[40] Abreu A. M. M., Lima J. M. B., Alves T. A. O impacto do álcool na mortalidade em acidentes de trânsito: uma questão de saúde pública. *Esc Anna Nery R Enferm.* 2006; 10 (1): 87-94.

[41] Souza M. F. M., Malta D. C., Conceição G. M. S., Silva M. M. A., Gazal-Carvalho C., Morais Neto O. L. Descriptive and trend analyses of land transport accidents for public policies in Brazil. *Epidemiol. Serv. Saúde.* 2007; 16 (1): 33-44.

In: Traffic Accidents and Safety: New Research ISBN: 978-1-63485-517-4
Editor: Garrett Bowman

Chapter 3

EVALUATION OF MOTORCYCLE RIDERS' BEHAVIOR WITH GLOBAL POSITIONING SYSTEM TECHNOLOGY

Panagiotis V. Lemonakis[1,*]***, George N. Botzoris***[2]***, Nikolaos E. Eliou***[1] ***and Theodoros E. Karakasidis***[1]

[1]University of Thessaly, Department of Civil Engineering, Greece
[2]Democritus University of Thrace,
Department of Civil Engineering, Greece

ABSTRACT

Countless research has been conducted during the last decades aiming to investigate the relationship between driver behavior and road features. The majority of the research is focused on passenger car speed, even though other modes of transport, for instance motorcycles, may be differently affected. In most of the cases researchers used pneumatic road tubes and video cameras to record vehicles' driving speeds and their vertical position. However, both pose risks to data validity due to human error and the inevitable effect of the equipment to drivers' behavior. The present investigation aims to bridge these gaps by evaluating motorcyclist's behavior and introducing a new methodology based on Global Positioning System (GPS). More specifically, the research is

[*] Corresponding author: University of Thessaly, Department of Civil Engineering, PedionAreos, GR-38334, Volos, Greece, Email: plemonak@gmail.com.

Vbox of Racelogic develops such benefits by combining a GPS data logger with a solid-state video recorder. The optional use of cameras results a graphical overlay, streamed onto an SD card while it is recording the following parameters as standard along with the video file: satellites, time, latitude, longitude, speed, heading, height and vertical speed. Table 1 is listing the specifications of the recording equipment.

Data loggers can record GPS, video and vehicle data and are ideally suited to motorsport due to their small weight, size and increased accuracy. Moreover, without fitting any other sensors, the measure of speed, track position, distance, lap time, lateral acceleration, longitudinal acceleration and height is feasible. Recording of such parameters can be particularly useful especially in cases where driving behavior is not approached exclusively in speed terms.

The videos, as well as the data files, are saved onto an SD card. The logging rate is 10 samples per second, which was considered as adequate enough to cover the needs of the study. As an example, an 8-gigabyte high capacity SD card, logging video on the highest quality setting was able to log approximately 160 minutes of video. Apparently, this is an approximation, as the size of the recorded video depended on what is being recorded. The motion, color and complexity of the subject matter affected the size of the video file created. It should also be mentioned that the size of the data file was particularly small, in comparison to the size of the video file.

The type of the recorded video file is MPEG-4 captured by 2 X AV cameras with integrated 12V power supplies and 2 X external microphones (the output sound is MP2 encoded video stream). The quality of the 24 bit color video file was either DVD 720 X 576 at 25 frames/sec or DVD 720 X 480 at 30 frames/sec.

In addition, by using a single recording system can make it possible to investigate multiple trajectories in multiple curves by a limited number of riders, since the various pieces of equipment are attached onto the vehicle instead of being on the road. Hence, aspects of participants' personality relevant to riding behavior e.g., demographics, accidents history and experience are known prior to the commencement of the experiments allowing the quantitative comparability of their performance.

In this manner both speed profiles (primary recording) and motorcycles' lateral position (originated from the recorded lateral and latitude data) accuracy are exclusively subject of the data logger specifications. Therefore, the mitigation of the recording equipment impact to riders' behavior is accomplished.

Table 1. Accuracies of Video Vbox

Output	Accuracy
Speed	± 0.20 Km/h
Distance	± 0.05%
Position	± 5 m
Height	± 10 m
Lateral acceleration	± 0.50%
Longitudinal acceleration	± 0.50%

Four software programs were used for processing the data recorded by Video VBox: Vbox Tools v2.2.2 b042 of RaceLogic, Excel 2010 of Microsoft, RapidDXF v4.0 of Delicad and AutoCAD 2007 of Autodesk.

The primary data files of *.vbo extension were opened with Vbox Tools which accompanied the recording equipment and converted to *.csv file extension. The created files contained the speed, distance and coordinates x,y for each one of the recorded points. Note that the points were recorded with a frequency of 10 Hz as much as the maximum frequency rate of Video Vbox. All of them were then numerical labeled in ascending order starting from 1 for the first point of each measurement.

Connecting the known recorded coordinates it was feasible to draw the trajectory of the riders. The software to do so was RapidDXF. The generated files (32 in total) of *.dxf extension were compatible with AutoCAD environment.

The next step was to draw a line, which in AutoCAD terms is called polyline that connects all of the points. Apparently the polylines corresponded to each one of the measurements. Finally, the plotted trajectories were georeferenced to EGSA 87 coordinates system. The background of the georeferenced map originated from http://gis.ktimanet.gr/wms/ktbasemap/ which is an open access website that provides orthophoto maps of the Greek territory. Based on the orthophoto maps, the boundaries and hence, the axis of the experimental roads were drawn. To simplify matters the axis of the road consisted of consecutive segments of tangents and arcs.

3. FIELD SITES AND EXPERIMENTS SETUP

Aiming to evaluate the proposed methodology, field measurements were conducted based on FESTA manual which discusses the design of the FOT

(Field Operational Test) in order to ensure scientific discipline and quality [19]. These measurements carried out taking into consideration the different parameters that may affect riders' behavior including different levels of experience (for this reason, the individuals chosen were not equally experienced), the existence of a pillion that not only affects the total weight of the rider/motorcycle system but also increases the driver's feeling of responsibility for his/her safety, as well as the different characteristics of the roads, such as the existence of signage and the magnitude of their curvature. It should be noted that no other parameters affecting driving behavior have been taken into consideration such as longitudinal inclination, super elevation, existence of shoulder, preceding tangents, vertical grades, etc.

Targeting to limit the variability and complexity of the riders' behavior, efforts were made so as to maintain similar conditions during each experiment. For this reason, factors such as lighting, weather conditions, temperature, presence of other users on the motorway during the measurements, condition of the motorcycle, etc. were alike throughout the execution of the field measurements and hence, the comparability of the data obtained from the recording equipment was ensured.

The selection of the experimental environments had to be based upon four primary conditions: the location, the type of the road, the weather conditions and finally, the time and date that the experiments would be conducted. All of these four conditions had to be common for all riders so that to record comparable data. In addition, the location of the experiments should ensure on one hand the constant function of the recording device, and on the other hand null traffic volumes throughout the experiments in order to achieve unaffected riding behavior by the participants. Finally, for purely practical purposes, the experimental environments sought close to the individuals' place of residence.

Taking into account the requirements mentioned above, two road networks selected; mountain Pelion in Magnesia (experiment 1) and the national road Thessaloniki – Evzonoi (experiment 2). The special features of each one are presented in sections 3.1 and 3.2.

3.1. Experiment 1: Correlation of Curve Radius with Speed – Classification of Road Environment Based on Motorcyclists' Behavior

The road network of Pelion consists exclusively of intensive curved rural roads, which vary depending on its geometrical characteristics, the presence of vertical/horizontal signage and the pavement condition. The traffic volumes are very limited during the autumn and winter months. Moreover, after the execution of several trial tests it was verified that the record device was working properly.

Through a more detailed investigation, the following road sections were determined as appropriate to carry out the field measurements:

- 1st road section: Part of road Afyssos – Afetai (39°16'30.24"B, 23°10'1.12"A to 39°16'53.69"B, 23°10'41.10"A). Length: approximately 2,300 m.
- 2nd road section: Part of road Milina – Lafkos (39°10'6.58"B, 23°13'43.97"A to 39°10'0.43"B, 23°14'21.94"A). Length: approximately 2,300 m.
- 3rd road section: Part of road Neohori – Kalamaki (39°18'43.98"B, 23°12'49.28"A to 39°19'23.41"B 23°11'45.51"A). Length: approximately 2,550 m.

The evaluation as well as the location of the experimental road sections are indicated in Table 2 and Figure 1 respectively.

Regarding the weather conditions and in order to restrict the parameters that affect the riding behavior of the participants, riders instructed to cease the measurements when the pavement was even slightly wet. The natural lighting level should be constant and hence, during cloudy or foggy days the measurements were ceased as well. In general, the instructions that were given to the riders did not allow the execution of the experiment in case any environmental or traffic conditions divert their regular riding behavior. It is also noted that the unimpeded approach to the curves ensured by succeeding null traffic volumes. For that purpose the measurements were conducted when the road was free from other road users.

Aiming at the investigation of the correlation between natural lighting and riding behavior, two different time periods were set for the execution of the experiment. The first one was set between 09:00 and 16:00 (constant natural lighting during autumn-daytime measurements) and the second one between 21:00 and 01:00 (nighttime measurements). Apparently, apart from the lighting conditions all the other environmental and weather conditions were equivalent for both time periods.

Another aim of the present experiment was the correlation between familiarity of the trajectory and riding behavior. For that purpose the participants were asked to ride each one of the routes six times during daytime and six times during nighttime. Finally, the riders were asked to repeat each route once more carrying a pillion in order to investigate how this condition influences their riding behavior since the presence of a pillion affects firstly the total weight of the system rider/motorcycle and secondly it increases the sense of responsibility of the rider for the pillion's safety. In total, two riders conducted 78 measurements as shown in Table 3.

Table 2. Evaluation of the experimental routes

Road section	Afyssos – Afetai	Milina – Lafkos	Neohori – Kalamaki
Curve radius range ($R_{min} \div R_{max}$)	11m ÷ 315m	24m ÷ 157m	49m ÷ 222m
Total pavement width	2.60m/direction	3.00m/direction	4.10m/direction
Horizontal signage	Absent	Limited to continuous single line on the centerline and the boundaries of the road	Yes
Vertical signage	Absent	Partially (3 danger signs)	Yes
Guard rails	Absent	Absent	Yes
Pavement condition	Extensive surfaces with cracks, grooves and subsidence	Several spots with transverse and longitudinal cracks, grooves and layering of bituminous seal	Excellent
Artificial lighting	Absent	Absent	Absent
Overall evaluation	Poor	Satisfactory	Excellent

Table 3. Amount and description of measurements

Condition	Number of routes	Number of repetitions	Number of riders	Total
Daytime	3	6	2	36
Nighttime	3	6	2	36
Pillion	3	1	2	6
Total amount of measurements:				78

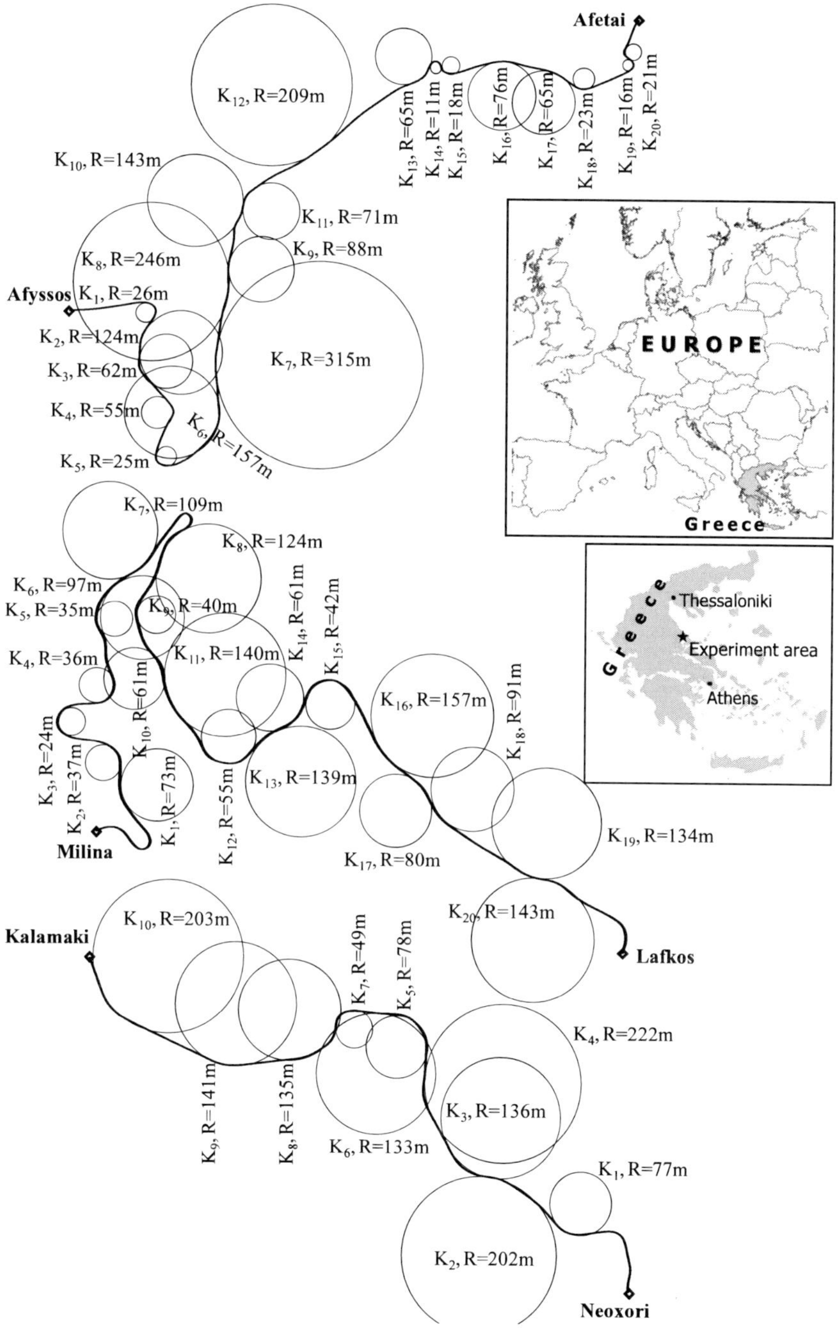

Figure 1. Experimental road layout.

3.2. Experiment 2: Correlation of Curve Radius and Curve Length with Speed – Motorcyclists' Behavior when Crossing Road Accesses

As stated before, experiment 2 was carried out in the national road Thessaloniki – Evzonoi and particularly in the road section from the north boundary of Polykastro settlement (41.003410, 22.570061) up to Mikrodasos settlement (41.067556, 22.575518), (Figure 2).

Although the experimental road is part of Greece's national road network, the geometric characteristics and the operational purposes that serves, classifies it to the rural road network. Twelve intersections and twenty curves that lie on the chosen road section were chosen for in-depth analysis.

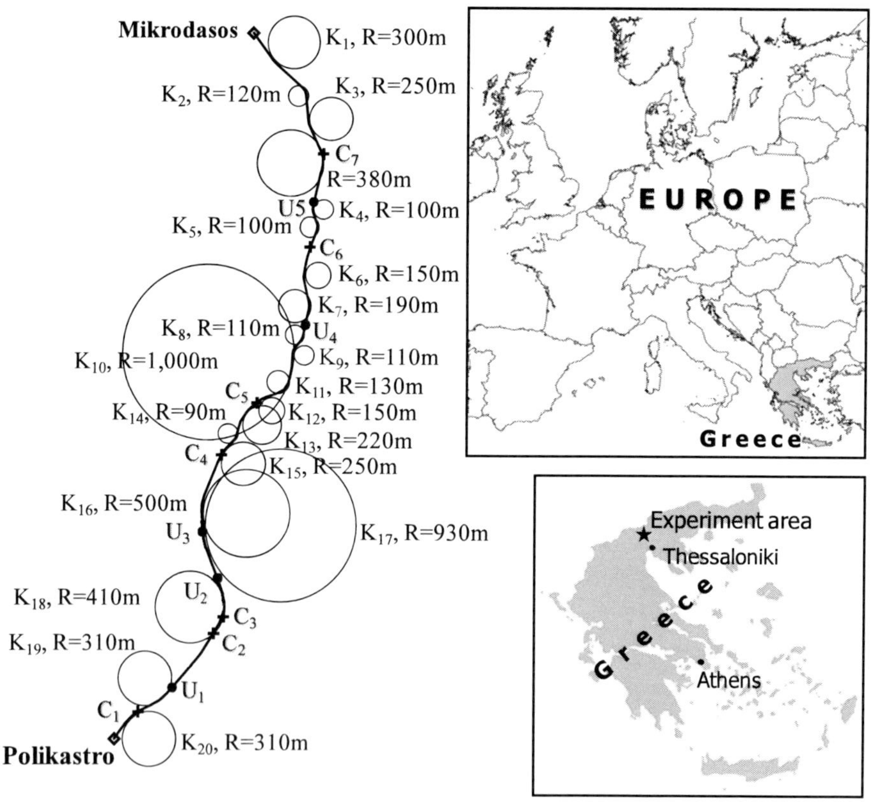

Figure 2. Experimental road layout (C: controlled accesses, U: uncontrolled accesses).

Table 4. Characteristics of accesses

	Controlled accesses							Uncontrolled accesses				
	C_1	C_2	C_3	C_4	C_5	C_6	C_7	U_1	U_2	U_3	U_4	U_5
Curve radius	380m	∞	550m	600m	250m	∞	250m	∞	∞	∞	∞	∞
Carriageway width	8.20m	8.20m	8.20m	8.20m	8.20m	8.20m	8.20m	8.20m	8.20m	8.20m	8.20m	8.20m
Vertical grade*	4.5%	+3.0%	+3.5%	0.0%	0.0%	0.0%	0.0%	+4.5%	+3.5%	0.0%	0.0%	0.0%
Condition of horizontal signage	Poor	Poor	Poor	Fair	Poor	Poor	Fair	Poor	Poor	Poor	Poor	Poor
Vertical signage	Good	Good	Excellent	Excellent	Excellent	Good	Excellent	Absent	Absent	Absent	Good	Absent
Pavement condition	Good	Poor	Good	Good	Good	Poor	Good	Good	Good	Good	Good	Good
Roadside land use	Fence	Trees	Trees	Trees	Gas station	Trees	Trees	Trees	Trees	Trees	Trees	Trees
Speed limit (km/h)	50	50	50	50	50	50	50	90	90	90	90	90

* positive sign stands for direction to Mikrodasos, see Figure 2.

Table 5. Characteristics of curves

Curve	Radius (m)	Centerline length (m)	Curve	Radius (m)	Centerline length (m)	Curve	Radius (m)	Centerline length (m)
K_1	300	59	K_8	110	40	K_{15}	250	99
K_2	120	70	K_9	110	51	K_{16}	500	132
K_3	250	34	K_{10}	1,000	164	K_{17}	930	138
K_4	100	38	K_{11}	130	129	K_{18}	410	264
K_5	100	51	K_{12}	150	72	K_{19}	310	142
K_6	150	39	K_{13}	220	47	K_{20}	310	160
K_7	190	57	K_{14}	90	48			

The characteristics of the 12 intersections and 20 curves encountered by the trial participants are shown in Table 4 and Table 5 respectively. Note that letter C stands for controlled accesses while letter U stands for uncontrolled ones.

In order to limit the parameters which affect the riding behavior of the individuals, the measurements commenced only when the pavement was clean and dry and the natural lighting adequate. Therefore, cloudy or precipitation days the measurements were ceased.

The experiment conducted by eight riders in two phases: first the participants were asked to travel on their own back and forth from Polykastro to Mikrodasos and second they repeated the same route carrying a pillion. Hence 32 measurements recorded by the eight riders for further analysis resulting 640 trajectories.

4. RECRUITMENT

Initially, three basic parameters had to be defined with regards to the participants' selection that would execute the field measurements; demographic criteria, riding experience and psychometric aspects of the riders [19]. The relevant data were obtained via questionnaires from a large number of candidates. The analysis of the questionnaires revealed the riders who met the experimental principles as described below.

The choice of the participants' gender was based on preceding researches which have shown that males are over-represented both in car and motorcycle accidents [20, 21], but also in the riding population even though they do not necessarily demonstrate riskier behaviors. Moreover, males constitute the typical rider gender and they can be recruited easier than the female ones.

Experience is also a significant factor that determines the level of risk taking behavior among riders. In most of the cases, there is a correlation between riding experience and age, since young riders are more inexperienced compared to the older ones. In order to reduce the probability of accident occurrence during the experiments, young and older riders were excluded, due to their high risk rates. Consequently, all participants had to have an actual riding experience of at least 5 years and should not be older than 50 years old. Aiming also to reduce the likelihood of traffic accidents, the sample of riders was biased towards riders with limited accident records. Furthermore, since one of the main objectives of the present research was to determine how the riding experience affects riding behavior, efforts were made to match the overall participants' features apart from their riding experience, which was selected to be considerably different.

Another issue that had to be dealt with was that the riders had to achieve a certain level of familiarity with the instrumented motorcycle. For that reason, prior to the execution of the field measurements, the riders were asked to ride the experimental motorcycle until they felt confident with its operation. It should also be noted that the demands for adequate handling were relatively increased due to the size and weight of the instrumented motorcycles.

4.1. Experiment 1: Correlation of Curve Radius with Speed – Classification of Road Environment Based on Motorcyclists' Behavior

Two male riders belonging at the same age group were selected to carry out the field measurements of experiment 1. None of them revealed any obvious reason of impaired riding ability while their riding experience levels were totally different. Moreover, they had common stay of residence, adjacent to the routes where the experiment was conducted and therefore, they both had similar familiarity with the experimental environment.

4.2. Experiment 2: Correlation of Curve Radius and Curve Length with Speed – Motorcyclists' Behavior when Crossing Road Accesses

The analysis of questionnaires reflecting demographic and behavioral aspects of several individuals led to the recruitment of the experiment with eight (four experienced and four inexperienced) coeval middle age male riders. All of them were non-disabled motorcycle riders, non-alcohol or drug consumers and hence their riding behavior was not even slightly impaired. Their riding experience levels varied although they all possessed motorcycles of similar size and weight with the one employed in the experiment. This fact along with the common place of residence ensured equal familiarity with the experimental conditions.

5. Instrumented Motorcycles

The selection of the motorcycles was a crucial element of the experiments since it was intensively correlated with the safety of the participants. The condition of Greek rural roads' pavement along with the need for convenience and adequate performance were of paramount importance. Especially in rural low friction roads, they had to be very comfortable and neutral motorcycles allowing absorbing pavement failures and leaving the rider unaffected to concentrate on the desirable trajectory. These principles are met on on/off motorcycles, often seen in the Greek provincial roads mainly because they give the rider the ability to move efficiently on asphalt and non-asphalt roads.

Motorcycle service technicians performed routine maintenance tasks before the commencement of the experiments. They also repaired the engines and the transmissions when needed and performed minor repairs to the body of the motorcycles. Thorough visual checks in a daily regime carried out by the participants in order to evaluate the condition of the motorcycles.

5.1. Experiment 1: Correlation of Curve Radius with Speed – Classification of Road Environment Based on Motorcyclists' Behavior

The instrumented motorcycle that was used to carry out the field measurements was a BMW F650. It is an on/off motorcycle, widespread on rural Greek roads, especially because of its ability to provide sufficient transport on asphalt, as well as on soil material surfaces. The displacement of the 4-stroke single cylinder engine is 652 cc with peak output of 48hp at 6,500rpm. Among other specifications, the instrumented motorcycle has top speed at 160 km/h, it accelerates from 0÷100 km/h at 5.2 seconds, it is equipped with a 5-speed gearbox, its seat height and weight is 82 cm and 199 kg respectively while both front and rear brakes consist of single disc.

5.2. Experiment 2: Correlation of Curve Radius and Curve length with Speed – Motorcyclists' Behavior when Crossing Road Accesses

The instrumented motorcycle chosen to carry out the field operational measurements was Honda XLV 650V Transalp, an on/off motorcycle, prevalent to the Greek rural roads mainly due to its effectively performance both in paved and non-paved roads. It carries a liquid cooled, four stroke engine of 647cc capacity that accelerates from low RPM's independently of the shifted gear. The high riding position which offers a great view of upcoming hazards along with the wide bars give great leverage in tight corners. Furthermore, the windshield protects efficiently from wind and flying debris up to the speed of 120 km/h providing comfort and safety to motorcycle's occupants. The relatively high weight (191 kg) is barely perceived due to the low gravity center. The steering is placed high, permitting great direction changes whereas the suspensions absorb effectively pavement failures.

6. Approaching Motorcycle Riders' Behavior at Curved Road Sections

A lot of research has been conducted during the last decades aiming to investigate the relationship between driver behavior and road features. The majority focuses on passenger's car speeds even though other modes of transport may be affected differently. The present section focuses on the investigation of motorcycle riders' behavior at curved road sections.

Within the context of the research a new methodology is proposed while field measurements were conducted, with the participation of two riders and the use of appropriate speed recording equipment based on a GPS system to confirm its efficiency. The measurements were conducted taking into account various factors that potentially influence riders' behavior such as the different light conditions, the difference on the riding experience level, the familiarity of the riders with the routes, the presence of pillion and the different road environments, such as width/condition of the road pavement, roadside land use, right/left -hand curves, etc. In the frame of the research we investigated the determination of the optimum regression curve between the curve radius' and the corresponding velocities based on a physical ground.

The research showed among others, that the regression curves could be used as a curve classification mean. Moreover, a significant variation was detected on the riders' behavior when carrying a pillion related to their experience levels.

6.1. Introduction

Multiple essays have been carried out during the last decades in the field of road safety in order to predict the relationship between driver behavior and road features (especially on horizontal curves). Many of these studies focus on creating analytical models expressing driver behavior in relation to the characteristics of the roads [22, 23, 24, 25]. In these models, driver behavior is expressed by the operating speed (V_{85}, that represents the 85th percentile speed), while the road characteristics are generally represented by the curvature change rate of the single curve or the horizontal curve radius, since it has been estimated that the magnitude of the radius of the horizontal curves is the most considerable factor that determines operational speed [26]. Nevertheless, the true effect of each individual geometric variable (e.g., curve radius, length of the curve, deflection angle and superelevation) is still not known precisely in quantitative terms [27].

As has already been stated, most models developed to date focus on passenger car speeds [8]. However, the speed behavior of motorcycles was studied by Perco [28], who evaluated the possibility to develop a motorcycle operating speed prediction model analyzing the relationships between the motorcycle and the passenger cars operating speed. Both motorcycle and vehicle speeds were collected using a Light Detection and Ranging (Lidar) gun while graphic as well as statistical analysis followed the measurements. The outcome of this research was the development of equation (1):

$$V_{85PTW} = 1.162 \cdot V_{85PC},\ R^2=0.94 \tag{1}$$

where:

V_{85PTW}:	the 85th percentile speed on tangent of power- two-wheelers (km/h),
V_{85PC}:	the 85th percentile speed on tangent of passenger cars (km/h),
R^2:	the coefficient of determination.

The subject in another study by Faezi et al. was to develop a speed prediction equation on horizontal curves using the geometric characteristics of the curves at 11 sites in exclusive motorcycles lane [29]. To achieve this objective, the speeds of motorcyclists were measured in exclusive motorcycle lanes in Malaysia using two devices; a portable laser speed detector and a digital video camera. The authors of this study by implementing linear regression procedure in order to identify the best fit combinations of the independent variables developed the model described by equation (2):

$$V_{85,\ curve} = 19.357 \cdot W - 0.394 \cdot \Delta + 0.654 \cdot T \tag{2}$$

where:

$V_{85,\ curve}$:	the 85th percentile motorcycle speed on horizontal curves,
W:	the total lane width,
Δ:	deflection angle,
T:	the length of tangent.

No other study relevant to motorcycle speed prediction equations has been carried out apart from the two afore-mentioned ones, at least to our knowledge. Therefore, the impact of the different light conditions, the different experience level, the familiarity with the road and the different road environment to drivers' behavior expressed in operating speed changes can only be observed in passenger cars studies.

The differences between driving behaviors when passenger car drivers' deal with right-hand (RH) and left-hand (LH) curves have been examined by several researchers. More specifically, the results of these investigations, as discussed by Fildes [30], showed that the drivers use different optical cues in RH and LH curves, have higher driving performance in RH curves and tolerate higher deviations from design course in RH in comparison to LH curves with similar features.

The fact that drivers respond in a different way to RH and LH curves also results in the study of Othman et al. [31], in which it is clearly indicated that the curve direction should be substantially studied in the design or redesign of the curves. It actually became apparent that the drivers and the vehicles are influenced by different infrastructure elements according to the curve direction.

It is known from the law of mechanics that the force resolution for the forces acting on a vehicle traversing a curve, leads to equation (3), [32]:

$$e + f = \frac{U^2}{R \cdot g} \tag{3}$$

where:

e: the superelevation,
f: the side friction factor,
R: the radius of curvature,
g: the acceleration due to gravity (9.81 m/sec^2),
U: the speed of the vehicle.

Equation 3 is based on the force balance for a point mass on a superelevated surface travelling at constant speed along a circular arc. However, when using equation (3), one of the basic problems encountered, as it was mentioned before, is the hypothesis that the radius is constant. Nevertheless, vehicles change their lane placement and trajectory and as a result the driven path might vary considerably from the curve radius. This was confirmed by many researchers who noticed that the trajectory can be different in a great extend from the design [33]. More specifically in curves with radius less than 150 m, drivers tended to increase the radius of their path from 0.6 m to 0.9 m in lateral position when driving inside curves. It should be noted that since the curve radius and the path radius vary, the calculation of the side friction factor constitute a complex problem, as shown by Wong and Nicholson [27] who suggested that the path instead of designing radius should be taken into account.

6.2. Data Processing

By implementing the procedure described in section 2, the calculation of the mean velocities in the curves for each one of the 78 different measurements was possible. More specifically, 50 curves were determined to further analysis; 20 curves located at route Afyssos – Afetai (9 curves were right-hand while 14 curves had radius R<100 m), 20 curves located at route Milina – Lafkos (10 curves were right-hand while 13 curves had radius R<100 m) and 10 curves located at route Neohori – Kalamaki (6 curves were right-hand while 3 curves had radius R<100 m) counting a sample size of 1,300 mean velocities, as shown in Table 6.

The next step of the data processing method was to determine the method to calculate the equations that correlate the recorded velocities with the corresponding radii of the horizontal curves as defined above. Previous studies have shown that linear regression can be used to predict operating speeds on circular curves and more specifically that the 85th percentile speeds on horizontal curves (the dependent variable) can be predicted using combinations of independent variables such as curve radius, length of the curve, deflection angle, and superelevation [34]. Apart from the afore-mentioned studies, it was evident that the ordinary least square regression was the most widespread model type among the various researchers that has been used in order to develop comprehensive speed prediction equations/models [8] and for that reason it was selected against other model types.

Table 6. Sample size for the evaluation of riders' behavior at curved road sections

	Rider 1						Rider 2						Total
Repetition	1st	2nd	3rd	4th	5th	6th	1st	2nd	3rd	4th	5th	6th	
Road section	Afyssos – Afetai												
Daytime	20	20	20	20	20	20	20	20	20	20	20	20	240
Nighttime	20	20	20	20	20	20	20	20	20	20	20	20	240
With pillion	20	-	-	-	-	-	20	-	-	-	-	-	40
Road section	Milina – Lafkos												
Daytime	20	20	20	20	20	20	20	20	20	20	20	20	240
Nighttime	20	20	20	20	20	20	20	20	20	20	20	20	240
With pillion	20	-	-	-	-	-	20	-	-	-	-	-	40
Road section	Neohori – Kalamaki												
Daytime	10	10	10	10	10	10	10	10	10	10	10	10	120
Nighttime	10	10	10	10	10	10	10	10	10	10	10	10	120
With pillion	10	-	-	-	-	-	10	-	-	-	-	-	20
Total amount of measurements													1,300

6.3. Results

The calculation of the mean velocities followed by the implementation of the ordinary least square regression method in order to determine the optimum regression curve between radius and speed that fitted better the distribution of the collected data.

Equation (3) presented above, can be rewritten as:

$$U = \sqrt{(e+f) \cdot R \cdot g} \tag{4}$$

Hence, the maximum speed of a vehicle traversing a curve in order not to invert or skid is given by the equation (5):

$$U = a\sqrt{R} \tag{5}$$

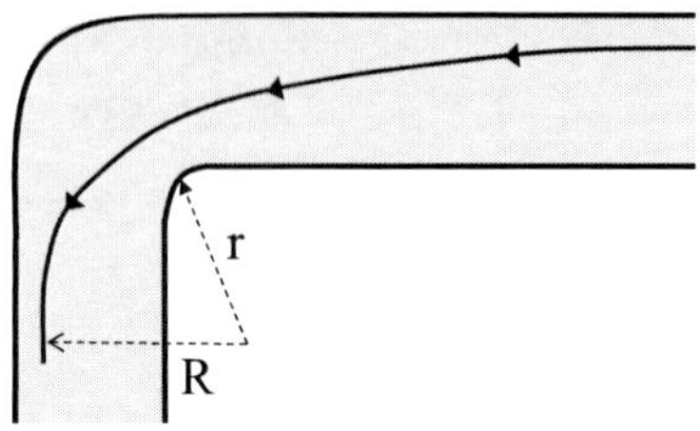

Figure 3. Trajectory of changing radius.

where:

- U: the speed of the vehicle.
- R: the radius of curvature,
- a: a coefficient depending on the center of gravity of the vehicle, the dimensionsof the vehicle, the side friction factor and the superelevation angle of the curve.

Therefore, it is essential for a driver to be aware of the fact that the centrifugal force F is proportional to the speed square and inversely proportional to the radius of the curve and hence side-slip phenomena might not appear when the rider accomplishes to increase the radius of his trajectory. This could be done when the riders cut the corner in such way that they exploit the largest part of the available pavement edges (Figure 3).

Accordingly, the rider traverses curved tracks with radius dissimilar than the radius of the curves at the center line of the road (geometric radius). Hence, the rider moves within left-hand (LH) curves between R and R+d (where d is the width of the lane) whereas in right-hand (RH) curves between R and R-d, assuming apparently that he remains at his lane throughout his movement within the curve. Therefore, the rider can achieve greater speeds in LH curves than in RH curves (since centrifugal force F is constant and hence, greater speed presuppose greater radius), given the fact that LH curves suggest greater radii. In this context, since the graphs represent speed against geometric radius, higher speeds are shifted to smaller radii in LH curves. This remark is particularly important in curves with small radii.

It is worth noting that equation (5) assumes the execution of *uniform circular motion* by the rider, which is not precisely applied due to the different speeds as well as to the different consecutive radiuses he traverses within the curve, resulting an error. Therefore equation (5) can be rewritten in a more general form as:

$$U = a \cdot R^b \tag{6}$$

Equation (6) compares favorably with equation (5) because on one hand it does not involve mandatory uniform circular motion (b not compulsorily equal to 0.50) on the other hand exponent b could be used as a criterion whether the motion of the rider approaches the uniform circular (the more b tends to 0.50 the more motion approaches uniform circular). Taking into consideration the afore-mentioned idea it was decided to implement ordinary least square regression to equation (6) that led to the calculation of the trend lines, the corresponding errors of coefficients a, b and the coefficient of determination R^2 for 64 different driving conditions. These conditions were oriented to investigate the impact of the different light conditions, the difference on the experience level, the familiarity of the riders with the routes, the presence of a pillion and the different road environments (e.g., LH and RH curves) to the participants riding behavior. The comparison of the various driving conditions performed by evaluating the behavior of the corresponding exponent b and coefficients a.

A thorough examination of RH curves showed that exponents b tend more to 0.50 indicating that the rider's movement approaches more a uniform circular motion (and hence the rider does not change his radius very much and he moves with lower speeds). Conversely in LH curves, exponent b presents values lower than 0.50 indicating that the rider can divert more from uniform circular motion by changing his speed and radius. This behavior might imply that in RH curves the riders probably move closer to the limit value of 0.50 (equation 5) than in LH curves. Moreover, it is interesting to note that the difference is also depicted in the coefficient a of equation (6). Therefore, it is obvious that in LH curves the coefficients a are greater than in RH curves. In general, for curves with radiuses above 100m and independently of the light conditions, both riders traverse RH curves with higher speeds than LH curves (Figures 4 to 7). The behavior is reversed for curves with radii below 100m, phenomenon that should be further investigated in the future.

An additional conclusion that came up from the analysis of the data is that in the routes with better geometric characteristics exponents b reduce while coefficients a increase. Hence in these routes the riders have greater range of curvature selection.

The evaluation of the calculated equations led to the conclusion that regression curves between speed and radius could be used as a classification tool of the road curves. Exponents b approaching 0.50 would indicate that the rider moves closer to the limit speed and hence such curves gather poor geometric characteristics. Similarly, the behavior of coefficient a is also related to the quality of the road. More specifically, comparing similar experimental conditions (e.g., behavior of experienced rider at nighttime), the value of coefficient a increases when the classification of the road increases.

Table 7. Equations of ordinary least square regression in the case of inexperienced rides

Conditions of the experiment					Trend line $U=a \cdot R^b$
Route classification	Light conditions	Repetitions	Presence of pillion	Curve direction	
Poor	Daylight	Avg. 1 to 3	No	Both	$U=8.427 \cdot R^{0.367}$
Poor	Daylight	Avg. 4 to 6	No	Both	$U=9.078 \cdot R^{0.338}$
Poor	Daylight	Avg. 1 to 6	No	Both	$U=8.739 \cdot R^{0.353}$
Poor	Nightlight	Avg. 1 to 3	No	Both	$U=8.973 \cdot R^{0.354}$
Poor	Nightlight	Avg. 4 to 6	No	Both	$U=8.756 \cdot R^{0.362}$
Poor	Nightlight	Avg. 1 to 6	No	Both	$U=8.866 \cdot R^{0.358}$
Satisfactory	Daylight	Avg. 1 to 3	No	Both	$U=12.29 \cdot R^{0.328}$
Satisfactory	Daylight	Avg. 4 to 6	No	Both	$U=13.50 \cdot R^{0.307}$
Satisfactory	Daylight	Avg. 1 to 6	No	Both	$U=12.88 \cdot R^{0.318}$
Satisfactory	Nightlight	Avg. 1 to 3	No	Both	$U=10.06 \cdot R^{0.335}$
Satisfactory	Nightlight	Avg. 4 to 6	No	Both	$U=12.46 \cdot R^{0.297}$
Satisfactory	Nightlight	Avg. 1 to 6	No	Both	$U=11.22 \cdot R^{0.316}$
Excellent	Daylight	Avg. 1 to 3	No	Both	$U=16.01 \cdot R^{0.288}$
Excellent	Daylight	Avg. 4 to 6	No	Both	$U=15.03 \cdot R^{0.313}$
Excellent	Daylight	Avg. 1 to 6	No	Both	$U=15.49 \cdot R^{0.301}$
Excellent	Nightlight	Avg. 1 to 3	No	Both	$U=14.81 \cdot R^{0.281}$
Excellent	Nightlight	Avg. 4 to 6	No	Both	$U=13.32 \cdot R^{0.303}$
Excellent	Nightlight	Avg. 1 to 6	No	Both	$U=14.04 \cdot R^{0.292}$
All routes	Daylight	Avg. 1 to 3	No	Both	$U=8.636 \cdot R^{0.393}$
All routes	Daylight	Avg. 4 to 6	No	Both	$U=8.733 \cdot R^{0.390}$
All routes	Daylight	Avg. 1 to 6	No	Both	$U=8.680 \cdot R^{0.392}$
All routes	Nightlight	Avg. 1 to 3	No	Both	$U=8.775 \cdot R^{0.369}$
All routes	Nightlight	Avg. 4 to 6	No	Both	$U=9.136 \cdot R^{0.365}$
All routes	Nightlight	Avg. 1 to 6	No	Both	$U=8.962 \cdot R^{0.367}$
Poor	Daylight		Yes	Both	$U=8.598 \cdot R^{0.321}$
Satisfactory	Daylight		Yes	Both	$U=13.21 \cdot R^{0.271}$
Excellent	Daylight		Yes	Both	$U=16.49 \cdot R^{0.268}$
All routes	Daylight		Yes	Both	$U=8.241 \cdot R^{0.369}$
All routes	Daylight	Avg. 1 to 6	No	Right-hand	$U=7.798 \cdot R^{0.416}$
All routes	Daylight	Avg. 1 to 6	No	Left-hand	$U=9.656 \cdot R^{0.367}$
All routes	Nightlight	Avg. 1 to 6	No	Right-hand	$U=8.430 \cdot R^{0.382}$
All routes	Nightlight	Avg. 1 to 6	No	Left-hand	$U=9.528 \cdot R^{0.352}$

Table 8. Equations of ordinary least square regression in the case of experienced rides

Conditions of the experiment					Trendline $U=a\cdot R^b$
Route classification	Light conditions	Repetitions	Presence of pillion	Curve direction	
Poor	Daylight	Avg. 1 to 3	No	Both	$U=8.596\cdot R^{0.357}$
Poor	Daylight	Avg. 4 to 6	No	Both	$U=8.281\cdot R^{0.367}$
Poor	Daylight	Avg. 1 to 6	No	Both	$U=8.439\cdot R^{0.362}$
Poor	Nightlight	Avg. 1 to 3	No	Both	$U=9.305\cdot R^{0.314}$
Poor	Nightlight	Avg. 4 to 6	No	Both	$U=9.142\cdot R^{0.329}$
Poor	Nightlight	Avg. 1 to 6	No	Both	$U=9.220\cdot R^{0.322}$
Satisfactory	Daylight	Avg. 1 to 3	No	Both	$U=12.67\cdot R^{0.312}$
Satisfactory	Daylight	Avg. 4 to 6	No	Both	$U=12.43\cdot R^{0.325}$
Satisfactory	Daylight	Avg. 1 to 6	No	Both	$U=12.55\cdot R^{0.318}$
Satisfactory	Nightlight	Avg. 1 to 3	No	Both	$U=12.92\cdot R^{0.288}$
Satisfactory	Nightlight	Avg. 4 to 6	No	Both	$U=12.28\cdot R^{0.326}$
Satisfactory	Nightlight	Avg. 1 to 6	No	Both	$U=12.56\cdot R^{0.308}$
Excellent	Daylight	Avg. 1 to 3	No	Both	$U=15.38\cdot R^{0.294}$
Excellent	Daylight	Avg. 4 to 6	No	Both	$U=13.06\cdot R^{0.332}$
Excellent	Daylight	Avg. 1 to 6	No	Both	$U=14.17\cdot R^{0.313}$
Excellent	Nightlight	Avg. 1 to 3	No	Both	$U=13.05\cdot R^{0.305}$
Excellent	Nightlight	Avg. 4 to 6	No	Both	$U=13.32\cdot R^{0.305}$
Excellent	Nightlight	Avg. 1 to 6	No	Both	$U=13.18\cdot R^{0.305}$
All routes	Daylight	Avg. 1 to 3	No	Both	$U=8.684\cdot R^{0.386}$
All routes	Daylight	Avg. 4 to 6	No	Both	$U=8.344\cdot R^{0.399}$
All routes	Daylight	Avg. 1 to 6	No	Both	$U=8.512\cdot R^{0.393}$
All routes	Nightlight	Avg. 1 to 3	No	Both	$U=9.087\cdot R^{0.353}$
All routes	Nightlight	Avg. 4 to 6	No	Both	$U=9.224\cdot R^{0.365}$
All routes	Nightlight	Avg. 1 to 6	No	Both	$U=9.154\cdot R^{0.359}$
Poor	Daylight		Yes	Both	$U=8.616\cdot R^{0.382}$
Satisfactory	Daylight		Yes	Both	$U=13.37\cdot R^{0.286}$
Excellent	Daylight		Yes	Both	$U=15.26\cdot R^{0.310}$
All routes	Daylight		Yes	Both	$U=8.644\cdot R^{0.394}$
All routes	Daylight	Avg. 1 to 6	No	Right-hand	$U=7.995\cdot R^{0.406}$
All routes	Daylight	Avg. 1 to 6	No	Left-hand	$U=9.054\cdot R^{0.379}$
All routes	Nightlight	Avg. 1 to 6	No	Right-hand	$U=7.852\cdot R^{0.393}$
All routes	Nightlight	Avg. 1 to 6	No	Left-hand	$U=10.650\cdot R^{0.326}$

Table 7 and Table 8 show (for experienced and inexperienced drivers respectively) the trend line (and the coefficients a, b) for the various riding conditions. It has to be noted that the coefficient of determination R^2 ranged from 0.745 to 0.973. The classification (poor, satisfactory and excellent) of the experimental road sections has been described in Table 2, whereas the layout has been illustrated in Figure 1.

Moreover, the mean speed of the experienced rider at the repetitions with the presence of the pillion is considerably higher than the corresponding speed of the inexperienced rider (Figure 8) implying that the experienced rider perceives more efficiently the benefit of the increased weight of the system motorcycle-rider-pillion which is accompanied by the increase of the side friction and therefore it permits higher speeds. This is clearly reflected in Figure 9, which shows the mean speed of the experienced rider for the various driving conditions where the highest speed is observed at the repetitions with the presence of the pillion.

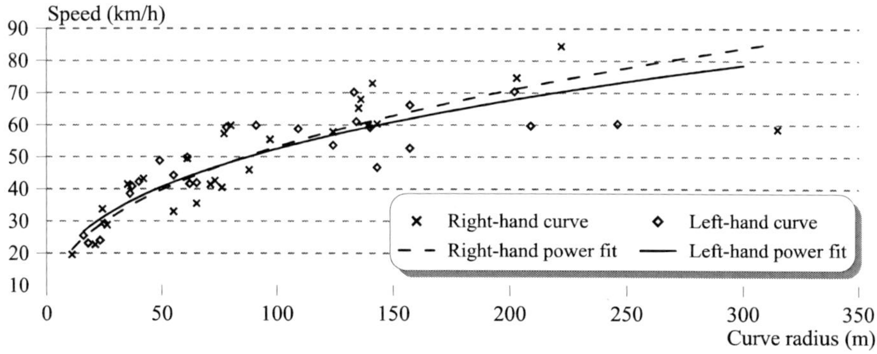

Figure 4. Speed vs. curve radius in all routes by *inexperienced* rider in right-hand and left-hand curves during *daylight*.

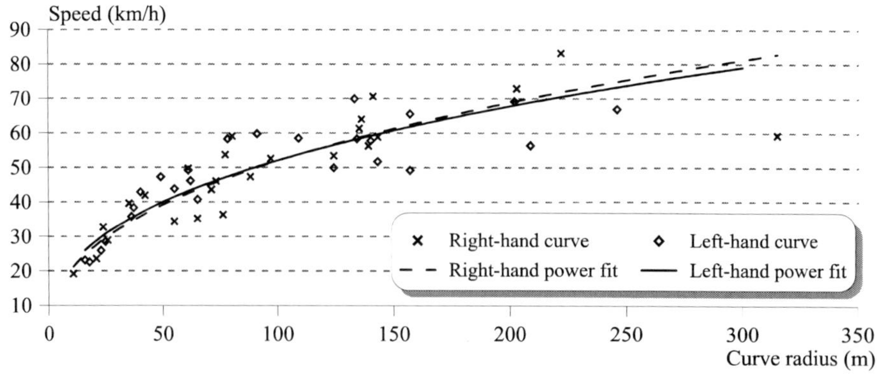

Figure 5. Speed vs. curve radius in all routes by *experienced* rider in right-hand and left-hand curves during *daylight*.

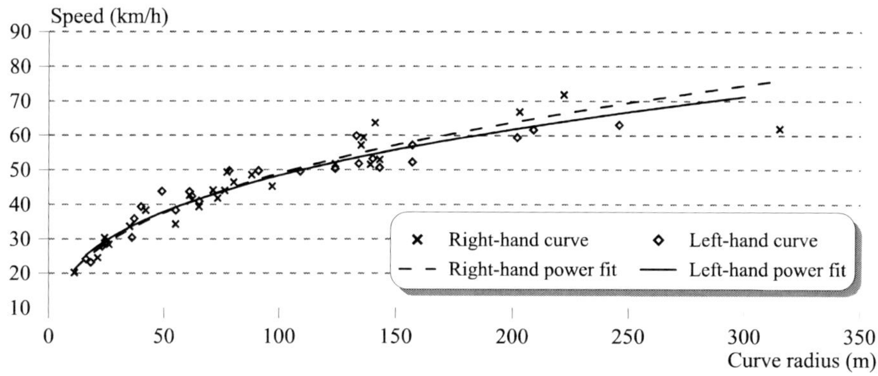

Figure 6. Speed vs. curve radius in all routes by *inexperienced* rider in right-hand and left-hand curves during *nightlight.*

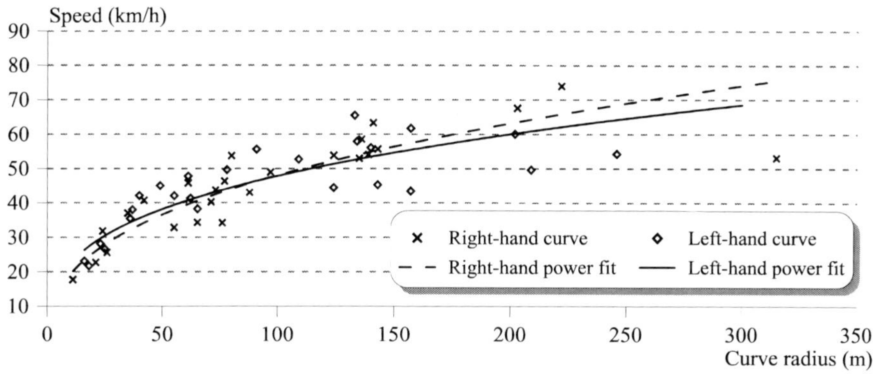

Figure 7. Speed vs. curve radius in all routes by *experienced* rider in right-hand and left-hand curves during *nightlight.*

On the contrary, the afore-mentioned benefit is not exploited by the inexperienced rider probably due to the sense of responsibility towards the pillion (Figure 10).

6.4. Concluding Remarks

Unlike the majority of the studies that have been carried out so far, where the velocities were recorded using a radar gun installed at a fixed point, usually in the middle of the curves forcing the researchers to install multiple radar guns in order to obtain speed data in multiple locations, the new methodology allows the investigation of motorcyclists' behavior in multiple locations since the riding performance data are recorded constantly throughout the trajectory of the rider.

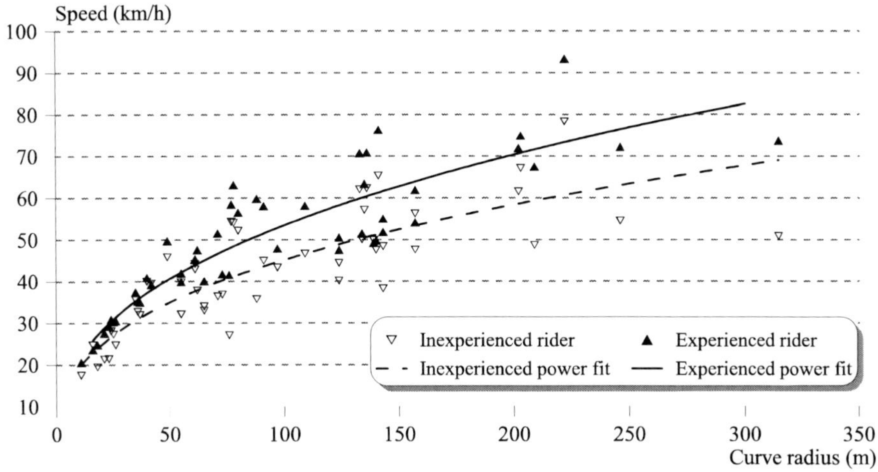

Figure 8. Speed vs. curve radius in all routes by *experienced* and *inexperienced* rider with the presence of *pillion*.

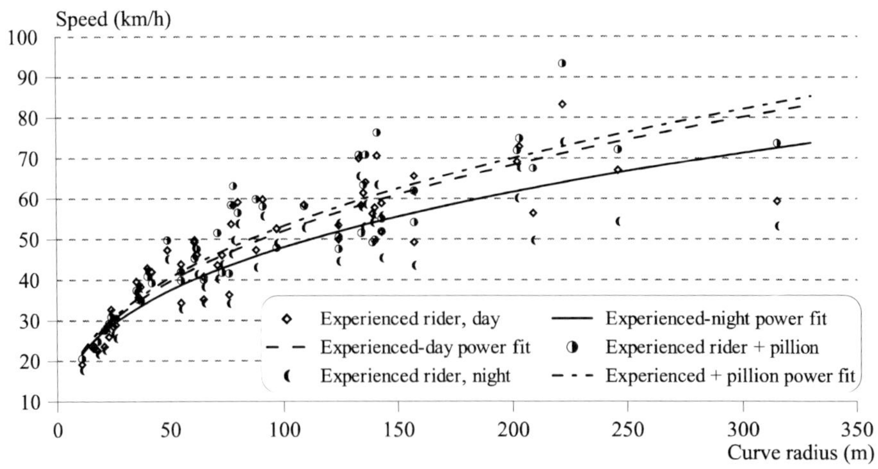

Figure 9. Speed vs. curve radius in all routes by *experienced* rider during *daylight*, *nightlight* and with the presence of *pillion*.

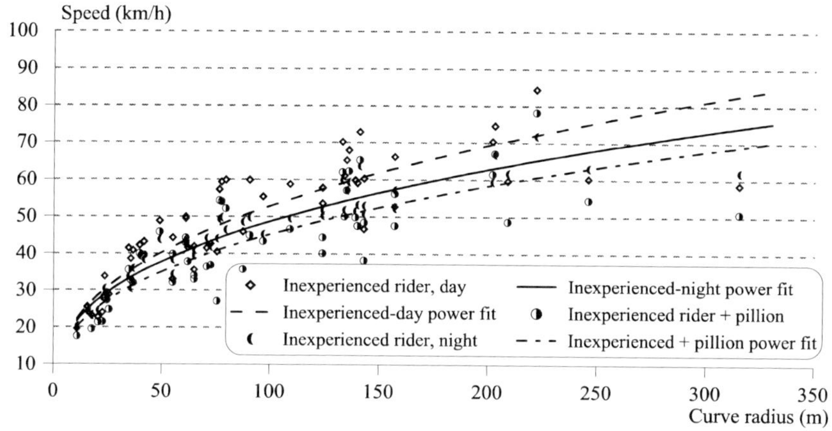

Figure 10. Speed vs. curve radius in all routes by *inexperienced* rider during *daylight*, *nightlight* and with the presence of *pillion*.

Therefore, the primary scope of the study is not to draw specific conclusions of the riding patterns observed but rather to demonstrate the feasibility of an alternative methodology in order to study riding behavior at curved road sections. The validation of the proposed methodology was performed by recruiting two motorcyclists, based on demographic, psychometric and experience criteria, that rode an instrumented bike in three different two lane rural roads under different driving conditions (i.e., presence of pillion, different light conditions). The ultimate objective was the determination of the optimum regression curve between the curve radius' and the corresponding velocities in a form of a power law of the form $U=a\cdot R^b$, which was accomplished with the implementation of the ordinary least square method. The afore-mentioned form was inspired from the fact that the speed of a body in a uniform circular motion would lead to a behavior b=0.5. Hence, the deviation of the exponent from this value would be indicative whether the motion approaches circular motion or not.

Within the limitations of the experiment (studied sites, number of participants, type of motorcycle) the conclusions drawn from the analysis of the recorded data, are presented below:

- Both riders travel with higher speeds in right-hand curves with radiuses above 100 m and independently of the light conditions, than in left hand curves. This conclusion reverses for curves with radiuses below 100 m, phenomenon that should be further investigated in the future.

- The data U, R could be fitted using a power law behavior $U=a \cdot R^b$ and the coefficient could be used as a classification tool of the road curves. A combination of decreased b value and increased a value leads to the conclusion that such curve gathers poor geometric characteristics.
- With regards to the presence of the pillion, the considerably higher mean speed of the experienced rider in comparison to the corresponding speed of the inexperienced rider was indisputable. Therefore, the experienced rider probably perceives more efficiently the benefit of the increased weight of the system motorcycle-rider-pillion which is accompanied by the increase of the side friction and therefore it permits higher speeds.

The results and conclusions presented above cannot be used as evaluation criteria of design consistency. Actually the scientific contribution of the present section should be considered as a first step on which further research should be based on incorporating a larger sample of motorcyclists in order to fine tune the proposed methodology, since there is no similar work examining riding patterns, at least to authors' knowledge, using GPS technology to obtain speed and track data for motorcycles.

7. Motorcycle Riders' Trajectory Assessment and Evaluation

Every driver follows a specific trajectory when moving through horizontal road curves, which is either wider or narrower than the centre line of the road. This driving line depends on the road environment characteristics (especially the curvature of the curve), the vehicle and the driver. Experienced drivers and especially motorcycle riders prefer to broaden their paths in order to achieve greater path curvature and hence, to reduce the applied centrifugal force. This behavior allows them to drive through horizontal curves faster and in a more comfortable way. The scope of the present section is to investigate riders' path while moving on curves. Within the context of the research, field measurements were conducted to a two lane rural road with the participation of eight riders and the use of an instrumented motorcycle. The research concluded that the trajectory of the riders is correlated with the radius and the length of the curve.

7.1. Literature Review

Numerous studies have shown that when speed control and driver's lateral positioning is not the optimum, dangerous driving conditions could be encountered in a curve [35, 36]. Although the increase in the lane width and the existence of shoulder have been suggested as measures mitigating dangerous conditions on a curve, it has been noted that these measures are connected with an increase in the operational speed of the riders, a fact that offsets any benefits initially gained [37].

The three main causes of accidents in curves are driver's lack of attention, insufficient entry speed and curvature perception as well as wrong lateral vehicle position [35]. In fact, determining the driver's real trajectory is a highly critical parameter since it shall define the required friction for safely driving through the curve. The initial assumption adopted by many researchers, i.e., that drivers' trajectory is identical to the axis of the road and hence, both road and trajectory curvature are similar, is unrealistic. Therefore, the calculation of the required side friction is erroneous.

It has been proven that in small curvature curves, drivers tend to increase the actual curvature of their trajectory (i.e., to cut the corner), [35, 38] and many researchers made a generalization on the basis of the abovementioned conclusion for all curves regardless of the size of the curvature [39]. Relatively recent research [10, 40] concluded that in small curvature radius, drivers tend to increase their trajectory radius so as to restrict the reduction in travel speed, while similar conclusions were made by Wonk [41] who pointed out that the increase in the driver's curvature was more possible to occur in curves with radius less than 150m.

The phenomenon where the curvature radius of the vehicle trajectory increases in horizontal curves has been recently confirmed not only for the inner but for the outer traffic lanes as well [42]. Finally, in the research conducted by Gawron and Ranney [43], 12 male drivers aged between 21÷55 were asked to drive in a simulator for two hours during which time their driving performance was recorded on 150 horizontal curves with radii varying between 188 and 356 feet (57 m÷109 m). The results have shown that the reduction to road curvature decreases the entry speed and increases the curvature of drivers' trajectory. Furthermore the drivers tended to take the wrong lateral position in curves with small curvature than in shorter curves.

After analyzing accident's data in various studies, there is strong evidence suggesting that the possibility of an accident is inversely proportional to the size of the curvature. Hence, the more the curvature increases, the less possible accidents occur and vice versa [35, 44, 45].

The research published by Fitzsimmons [10] makes reference to papers investigating vehicle trajectory in horizontal curves in roads with one lane per direction. The researchers divided drivers' trajectories in six categories (Figure 11) depending on the extent to which they were following the axis of the road. They concluded that the *"Normal"* and *"Cutting"* type trajectories are the most frequent [46].

Although there is extensive literature on the trajectories of vehicles in horizontal curves, not much research focuses on the behavior of motorcycle riders. The present research aims to address this gap in the literature proposing a new methodology for comparing the actual trajectory of the riders in relation to the curved sections of a road while at the same time it provides the basis for conclusions that combine the curvature of the curves with the length of the respective circular arc. For this reason, field operational tests have been designed and performed on a two lane rural road with the use of special recording equipment.

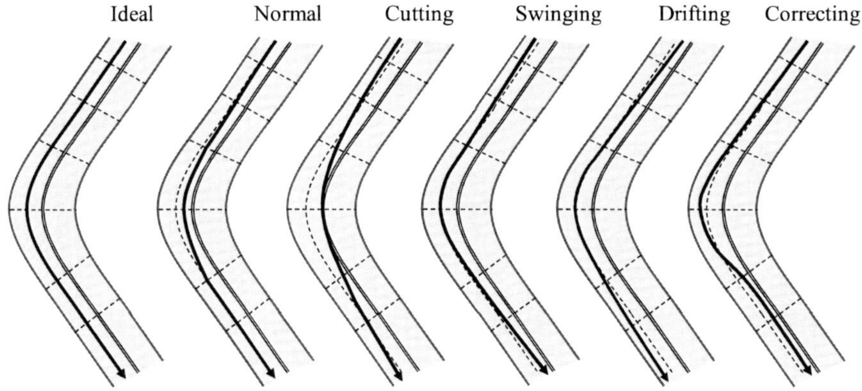

Figure 11. Categorization of the outer traffic lane trajectories.

7.2. Data Processing

Based on the preceded literature review, it became clear that the trajectories' curvature of the riders during their motion in curves is not identical to the radius of the curvature of the curve, and hence drivers move in a way that could either increase or reduce the difference between the actual and theoretical trajectory. In the first case, there can be no safety issue related to the lateral friction requirements as opposed to the second case when the drivers have to traverse a curve that is designed to provide lower values.

Previous researchers determined the critical radius of the various trajectories, by calculating the radii of the circles defined by three consecutive points of the trajectory. The minimum of these radii defined the critical one based on which the side friction requirement was calculated [39]. It was proven that the minimum - and therefore critical trajectory - appeared anywhere within the curve. The recording of the trajectory with a curvature smaller than that of the curve at any part of it thereof was calculated in other researches [45], which emphasized on the critical role of such event for the safe passage of drivers through curves.

The radius of 20 curves calculated and further studied by implementing the method described in section 2. The next step of the data process method was the calculation of trajectories' curvature. For this purpose, the least squares methodology was implemented aiming to determine the circle equation that best describes the experimental data, i.e., the coordinates X, Y of the trajectories' points that lie within the curves [47]. It should be noted that by this way only a representative curvature value of the curved segments was estimated and not the actual curvature thereof.

7.3. Results

Charts of the path radius (R_{path}), curve radius (R_{road}) and lengths of the circular arcs (curve length) followed the calculation of the trajectories and road curvature. From the analysis of these charts, it became clear that the riders did not follow the theoretical path in the middle of the lane. Moreover, strong indications regarding the correlation between the radius of the path and the radius of the curve (correlation factor $R^2 \cong 0.85$) for all experimental conditions (measurements with or without the pillion) for all riders were revealed. Indicatively, Figure 12 illustrates the correlation between the paths' and the curves' radii from Mikrodasos to Polykastro for measurements taken both with and without a pillion. The bold line depicts the event on which the path radius coincides with the curve radius ($R_{road} = R_{path}$).

As has already been mentioned in the introduction, the critical trajectories are those for which curvature is smaller than the radius of the curve. Data processing showed that riders traversed two specific curves with a path curvature smaller than that of the curve and hence, these two curves seem to establish conditions for eventual accident due to insufficient lateral friction.

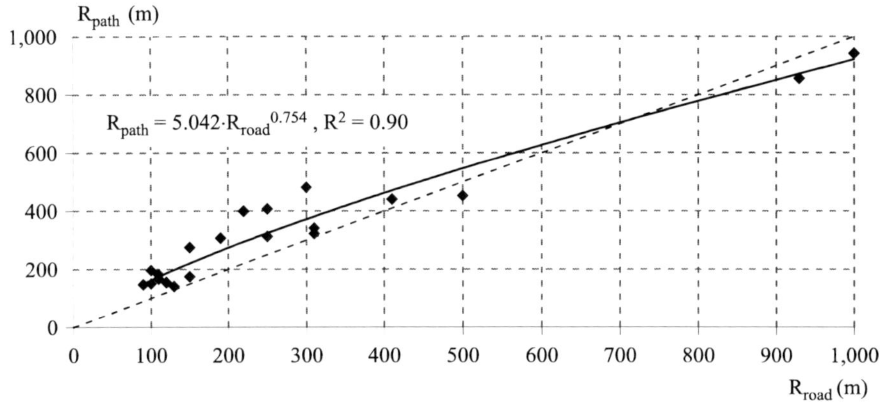

Figure 12.Correlation of the path radius (R_{path}) with the curve radius (R_{road}) at the route Mikrodasos – Polykastro.

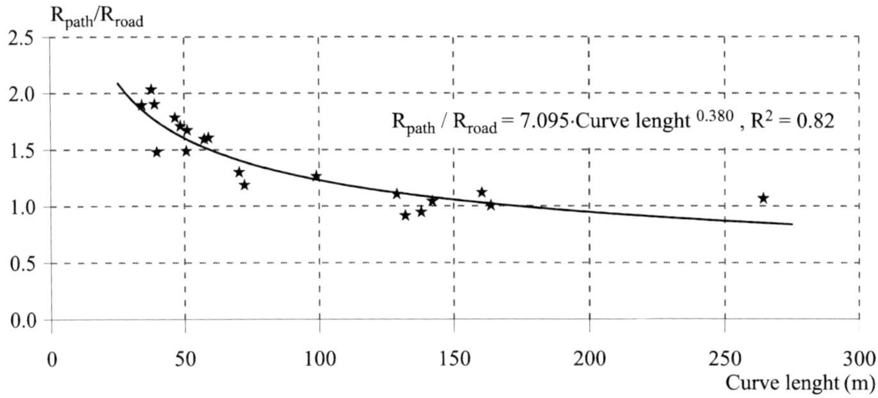

Figure 13. Correlation of the circular arc curve length to the ratio path radius / curve radius (R_{path}/R_{road}) at the Mikrodasos – Polykastro route with a pillion.

Furthermore, a clear conclusion was made regarding the impact of riders' behavior while carrying a pillion to the curvature of their trajectory. This fact did not confirm the initial assessments according to which riders were expected to take a more conservative path due to their increased sense of responsibility. More particularly, in the Polykastro – Mikrodasos route, riders without a pillion increased their average curvature by 39% compared to the radius of the curves while the respective percentage driving with a pillion recorded a small increase of 1%. Similar results observed during the reverse route.

Finally, aiming to establish the correlation of the length of the circular arc curves with the trajectories and road curvature, charts depicting the length of the circular arc against the ratio R_{path}/R_{road} created. From these charts, it is clear that riders deviate more than the theoretical trajectory into short length curves. Indicatively, Figure 13 shows the relative chart of the Mikrodasos – Polykastro route with the presence of a pillion.

7.4. Concluding Remarks

According to the literature, drivers traversing curves tend to alter their trajectory compared to the theoretical trajectory set by the designer. The goal is to enhance the perceived safety and comfort since the increase in the trajectory curvature results a reduction in the centrifugal force. Therefore, they can ride faster improving their performance.

Although there is extensive literature dealing with the trajectory of car drivers in curves, the same does not apply for motorcycle riders. This research aims to address this gap as it investigates the trajectories of motorcycle riders in curved road sections. For this purpose, field measurements were performed on a two lane rural road on both directions with the participation of 8 riders and the use of an instrumented motorcycle. The riders were asked to drive with and without a pillion. Special recording equipment as well as the application of an innovating processing methodology, led to the following conclusions:

- There is strong correlation between the radius of the trajectory and the radius of the curve for both conditions (with and without a pillion). This conclusion applies to all riders.
- Although in general riders increased their curvature compared to the curvature of the road, in two specific curves, the opposite behavior was observed. In fact, this was recorded in both directions.
- There was no difference in the behavior of riders in the event of carrying a pillion as regards to the curvature of their trajectories, although it was initially assumed that a differentiation would be evident because of the increased sense of responsibility that riders were expected to have when riding carrying a pillion.

- The charts of the ratio of curvature trajectory to the curvature of the curves and the length of the circular arc curves showed that the increase in the curvature of the trajectory is greater in curves with lesser lengths.

In order to confirm the aforementioned trends and hence generalize the conclusions drawn from the present research, more measurements must take place with the attendance of a larger sample of riders in multiple road types. Ideally the experimental road sections must be accurately plotted prior to the commencement of the measurements in order to accomplish precise positioning of riders' trajectories with respect to the road boundary lines.

8. Investigation of Road Accesses Effect to Motorcycle Riders' Behavior

The objective of the present section is to contribute to the enquiry of the effect of road accesses to roadside land uses in motorcycle riders' behavior. Within the context of the research, field measurements were conducted, with the participation of eight riders and the use of proper instrumented motorcycle as described in section 7. The research showed that speed and traffic offences adjacent to road accesses are higher for the experienced riders. It is worth noting that the conclusions resulted are a record of trends in the influence of roadside access to the behavior of riders since the generalization of these trends requires greater statistical sample.

8.1. Literature Review

The term access stands for the general connection of a public road with a private property (land, parcel) through a particular or non-particular construction (e.g., road, passage, trench, shoulder and walkway), [48]. The connections of private roads with public ones are also characterized as accesses but not the road meetings and junctions of public roads, which appertain to intersections. Lastly intersection is the area where two or more roads connect or intersect [48].

The significance of roadside land uses traffic connection is broader than that of access and consists apart from the features of the approach/exit construction to the roadside land use, the traffic data of the access as well, e.g., signage, left turns in united and separated road pavements (openings in medians and exclusive turn lanes), alternative routes instead of left turns, etc. On a case-by-case basis, the terms traffic connection and traffic access are used synonymously. The wider meaning of the traffic connection term from the operation point of view includes also the intersections. Hence, in the present section the term access includes the intersections of the rural network as well.

Previous research concluded that the type of the intersection is a crucial element to riders' safety. Hurt et al. [49] and de Lapparent [50] pointed out that severe or fatal accidents occur more often in intersections than in parts of the road with no intersections at all. Moreover, the key cause of traffic accidents is the failure to yield right-of-way. In such type of accidents, a vehicle approaches a junction from a road which lies on the right side of an arterial with regard to its driving direction, colliding or deflecting a motorcycle traveling on the arterial [49, 50, 51].

The outcome from another research relevant to motorcycle accidents is that the failure to yield the right of way (intersections constitute typical examples) is the principal cause of traffic accidents involving motorcycle riders [53]. The car drivers often report after the accidents that they checked but failed to perceive the existence of the motorcycle. However, it is very likely not to have checked at all or checked at the opposite direction [52].

In a deep investigation of several traffic accidents revealed that passenger vehicle drivers' failure to yield the right of way is the premier crash related factor of two vehicle motorcycle accidents [54]. In Australia, Williams and Hoffmann [55, 56] reviewed 1,508 motorcycle accidents. The outcome of the investigation was that the insufficient motorcycles' conspicuity was a co-factor in 64.5% of car-motorcycles accidents and the sole factor in the 21.0% of them. Quite interestingly the outcome of Smith's research showed that the car drivers perceive on time powered two wheelers presence during nighttime probably due to motorcycles' lights [57].

Wulf et al. [58] concluded that the responsibility in car-motorcycles collisions usually lies on the car driver. The most common type of collisions concerns failure to give the right of way because the car driver failed to perceive on time the presence of the motorcycle. According to another study [59], accidents in junctions represent 17% of fatal accidents and 30% of the total traffic accidents. It has to be noted that the majority concerns mopeds. Further investigation of these accidents showed that 87% referred to failure to yield the right of way from the driver of the four wheel vehicle while the remaining 13% the failure lies on the rider. This evidence suggests that drivers' instead of riders' behavior in junctions is the principal cause of accidents, in car-motorcycle type of accidents.

A research of ACEM (Association des Constructeurs Européens de Motocycles) indicates that half of the motorcycles accidents occur in junctions [60]. The root cause in the afore mentioned research is the limited cognitive conspicuity of the motorcycles due to its relatively less frontal area compared to the four wheel vehicles. Significant parameter is the fact that the eyes of a rider are higher than those of a driver and hence rider's optimum line of vision is different. Therefore, riders perceive approaching cars in intersections earlier than the drivers of the cars perceive the motorcycles. Lastly the inappropriate speed appears to affect the severity of injury on traffic accidents [60, 61], especially in uncontrolled intersections [62].

In the framework of the present study, field operational tests carried out under different conditions in order to investigate the behavior of motorcycle riders' at rural roads accesses. Ultimate goal was the determination of the accesses' characteristics that affect most riders' behavior. It should be noted that the conclusions drawn merely depict the trends of riders' behavior on rural accesses, meaning that the generalization of these trends require greater statistical sample.

8.2. Data Processing

The process of the data recorded at Video Vbox was described in a detailed manner in section 7.2. The outcome was the selection of 12 accesses that were chosen for further analysis. These were depicted on the map and labeled with letter C or U for controlled or uncontrolled ones respectively. A zone of 50 m before and after each access, as shown in Figure 2, was then determined, in which the speed profiles and therefore the mean speed of all riders were known.

8.3. Results

The repeating implementation of the method described in section 2 adapted in accesses instead of curves, led to the calculation of the mean speed of all riders within the 100m zone at each access. The seven controlled (C1÷C7) and the five uncontrolled (U1÷U5) accesses were analyzed under the various conditions with regards to the mean riding speed. Particularly, charts incorporating experience level and presence of pillion impact to the mean speed were constructed. Lastly it was investigated in which extent the riders obeyed to the posted speed limits.

In order to accomplish a more comprehensive analysis of the results, the two opposite directions were processed separately. Consequently, the relevant results and conclusions are presented in different paragraphs.

8.3.1. Direction Polykastro to Mikrodasos (see Figure 2)

An independent-samples t-test indicated that the experienced riders without the presence of pillion speed more (mean=86.17, std. deviation=6.84) than the inexperienced riders (mean=72.80, std. deviation=7.41), ($t(24)=4.78$, $p=0.00<0.05$ for equal variances as Lavene's test indicated $F=0.19$ and $p=0.66>0.05$), (Table 9). This trend is also applicable in the measurements with the presence of a pillion (experienced riders: mean=82.33 and std. deviation=6.57, inexperienced riders: mean=76.22 and std. deviation=6.34, independent-samples t-test: $t(24)=2.41$, $p=0.02<0.05$ for equal variances as Lavene's test indicated $F=0.06$, $p=0.81>0.05$).

Conversely, experienced riders tend to reduce speed when they carry a pillion, probably due to the cognitive sense of responsibility they bear (without pillion: mean=86.17 and std. deviation=6.84, with pillion: mean=82.33 and std. deviation=6.57, paired-samples t-test: $t(12)=3.16$, $p=0.01<0.05$), (Table 9). On the other hand, inexperienced riders seem to increase their speed when they carry a pillion (without pillion: mean=72.80 and std. deviation=7.41, with pillion: mean=76.22 and std. deviation=6.34, paired-samples t-test: $t(12)=-2{,}63$, $p=0.02<0.05$). A conceivable explanation of such trend is their ignorance of the risks involved in such event.

Another conclusion that revealed was the tendency of the riders to speed more in uncontrolled accesses (Table 10). In fact, the difference of the mean riding speed for both experienced and inexperienced riders in uncontrolled accesses (mean=83.75 and std. deviation=6.18) is statistically significant greater (independent-samples t-test: t(46)=-3,24, $p=0.00<0.05$ for equal variances as Lavene's test indicated $F=2.16$, $p=0.15>0{,}05$) compared to the mean speeds in controlled accesses (mean=76.26 and std. deviation=8.90). Therefore, either the riders failed to perceive on time the presence of an access and adjust their riding speed or they underestimated the dangers involved in uncontrolled accesses.

Table 9. Mean speed (in km/h) per access for experienced and inexperienced riders with and without pillion at the Polykastro – Mikrodasos route

	Controlled accesses							Uncontrolled accesses					Mean speed
	C_1	C_2	C_3	C_4	C_5	C_6	C_7	U_1	U_2	U_3	U_4	U_5	
Inexperienced riders													
Without pillion	60.41	78.07	74.91	63.90	60.94	75.60	66.46	77.43	81.48	80.75	79.37	74.25	72.80
With pillion	70.81	75.29	72.35	75.61	66.44	78.54	69.67	77.52	89.70	86.00	78.97	73.70	76.22
Experienced riders													
Without pillion	72.07	95.27	90.46	84.99	79.18	82.50	83.75	81.74	95.52	93.59	91.16	83.87	86.17
With pillion	75.31	91.05	86.00	74.44	68.26	83.81	79.10	84.01	89.47	89.23	84.50	82.75	82.33

Of particular interest is also the attitude of the riders towards posted speed limits especially as they approach an access. It should be noted that the posted speed limit on the experimental road was 90 km/h including uncontrolled accesses and 50 km/h on the controlled ones. As shown in Figure 14, both experienced and inexperienced riders disobey to the maximum speed limit in controlled accesses while in the uncontrolled ones only the experienced riders without carrying a pillion break the limit of 90 km/h.

Table 10. Mean speed (in km/h) per type of access for experienced and inexperienced riders with and without pillion at the Polykastro – Mikrodasos route

	Without pillion		With pillion	
	Controlled accesses ($C_1 \div C_7$)	Uncontrolled accesses ($U_1 \div U_5$)	Controlled accesses ($C_1 \div C_7$)	Uncontrolled accesses ($U_1 \div U_5$)
Experienced riders	84.03	89.18	79.71	85.99
Inexperienced riders	68.61	78.66	72.67	81.18

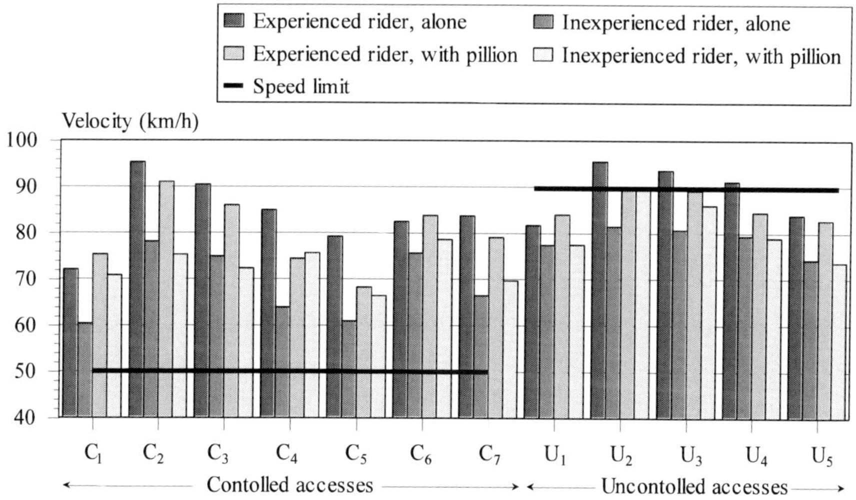

Figure 14. Riders' (with and without pillion) speeds per access in comparison with the posted speed limit at the Polykastro – Mikrodasos route.

8.3.2. Direction Mikrodasos to Polykastro (see Figure 2)

The results as well as the statistical analysis presented in previous section are similar for the opposite direction. The experienced riders speed more compared to the inexperienced ones in all accesses controlled or not and regardless of carrying a pillion or not. They are also speeding more when they travel on their own while respective trend was not ascertained to the inexperienced riders, as shown in Table 11. Similarly to the conclusion drawn previously for the opposite direction (Polykastro – Mikrodasos), all drivers speed more at uncontrolled accesses either they carry a pillion or not (Table 12). Lastly, both inexperienced but mainly the experienced riders travel with considerable greater speed compared to the posted limit in controlled accesses. However in uncontrolled accesses only the experienced riders carrying a pillion tend to break the posted speed limit as clearly illustrated in Figure 15.

Table 12. Mean speed (in km/h) per type of access for experienced and inexperienced riders with and without pillion at the Mikrodasos – Polykastro route

	Without pillion		With pillion	
	Controlled accesses ($C_1 \div C_7$)	Uncontrolled accesses ($U_1 \div U_5$)	Controlled accesses ($C_1 \div C_7$)	Uncontrolled accesses ($U_1 \div U_5$)
Experienced riders	83.17	92.65	80.21	85.57
Inexperienced riders	71.84	79.10	74.25	79.32

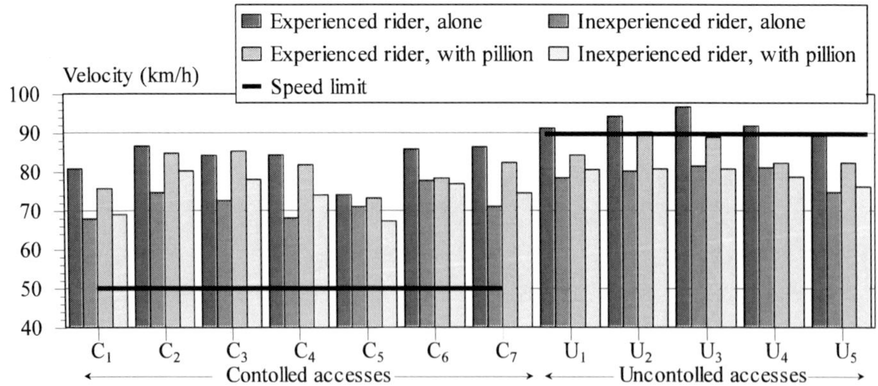

Figure 15. Riders' (with and without pillion) speeds per access in comparison with the posted speed limit at the Mikrodasos – Polykastro route.

Table 11. Mean speed (in km/h) per access for experienced and inexperienced riders with and without pillion at the Mikrodasos –Polykastro route

	Controlled accesses							Uncontrolled accesses					Mean speed
	C_1	C_2	C_3	C_4	C_5	C_6	C_7	U_1	U_2	U_3	U_4	U_5	
Inexperienced riders													
Without pillion	67.79	74.63	72.64	68.07	70.97	77.79	71.01	78.39	80.07	81.42	80.99	74.65	74.87
With pillion	68.92	80.23	78.03	73.99	67.28	76.88	74.45	80.61	80.65	80.65	78.58	76.12	76.36
Experienced riders													
Without pillion	80.74	86.57	84.25	84.32	74.03	85.86	86.41	91.23	94.27	96.64	91.81	89.30	87.12
With pillion	75.68	84.80	85.31	81.80	73.14	78.39	82.38	84.34	90.20	88.90	82.18	82.23	82.44

8.4. Concluding Remarks

According to the results of the statistical analysis presented in section 8.3, the following trends can be identified:

- The experienced riders travel with greater speed in all accesses (controlled or not) and under any conditions in both directions.
- The experienced riders speed is higher when they do not carry a pillion.
- In both directions the riders speed more at the uncontrolled accesses and hence they fail to perceive on time the presence of the access or they underestimate the risks involved in them. This trend concerns all riders either carrying a pillion or not.
- Riding in excess of the speed limit was recorded for all riders. Particularly their tendency is to break the posted speed limit in the controlled intersections. Nevertheless in uncontrolled accesses, only experienced riders traveling on their own disobeyed the posted speed limit.

CONCLUSION

The majority of the studies carried out so far, utilized radar guns, cameras and pneumatic road tubes to obtain speed and position data. Hence, the investigation of multiple sites required to install multiple sets of equipment in multiple locations. Unlike to the preceding practice, the new methodology proposed in the present study, allows the investigation of motorcyclists' behavior in multiple locations at once, since the riding performance data (e.g., speed, position) are recorded constantly throughout the trajectory of the rider.

Therefore, the primary scope of the chapter is not to draw specific conclusions of the riding patterns observed but rather to demonstrate the feasibility of an alternative methodology in order to study riding behavior under various conditions. The validation of the proposed methodology was performed conducting two experiments, the main conclusions of which are the following:

- The data U, R (U, R stand for speed and curve radius respectively) could be fitted using a power law behavior $U=a\cdot R^b$ and the coefficient could be used as a classification tool of the road curves. A combination of decreased b value and increased a value leads to the conclusion that such curve gathers poor geometric characteristics.

- The experienced riders probably perceive more efficiently the benefit of the increased weight of the system motorcycle-rider-pillion which is accompanied by the increase of the side friction and therefore it permits higher travelling speeds.
- There is strong correlation between the radius of the trajectory and the radius of the curve for both conditions (with and without a pillion). This conclusion applies to all riders.
- There is no difference in the behavior of riders and the event of carrying a pillion as regards to the curvature of their trajectories, although it was initially assumed that a differentiation would be evident because of the increased sense of responsibility that riders were expected to have when riding carrying a pillion.
- The increase in the curvature of the trajectory is greater in curves with lesser lengths.
- The experienced riders travel with greater speed in all accesses (controlled or not) and under any conditions in both directions.
- The experienced riders speed more when they do not carry a pillion.
- In both directions the riders speed more at the uncontrolled accesses and hence they fail to perceive on time the presence of the access or they underestimate the risks involved in them. This trend concerns all riders either carrying a pillion or not.
- Riding in excess of the speed limit recorded for all riders. Particularly their tendency is to break the posted speed limit in the controlled intersections. Nevertheless, in uncontrolled accesses only experienced riders traveling on their own disobeyed the posted speed limit.

References

[1] Haworth, N., Greig, K. and Nielson, A. (2009). A comparison of risk taking in moped and motorcycle crashes. *Transportation Research Record: Journal of the Transportation Research Board, 2140*, 182-187.

[2] Quddus, M.A., Noland, R.B. and Cin, H.C. (2002). An analysis of motorcycle injury and vehicle damage severity using ordered probit models. *Journal of Safety Research, 33*(4), 445-462.

[3] National Highway Traffic Safety Administration (NHTSA). *State blood alcohol concentration testing and reporting for drivers involved in fatal crashes: Current practices, results, and strategies, 1997-2009.* Washington D.C.: US Department of Transportation, 2012.

[4] National Highway Traffic Safety Administration (NHTSA). *An analysis of motorcycle helmet use in fatal crashes.* Washington D.C.: US Department of Transportation, 2008.

[5] Ogunmodede, T.A, Adio, G., Ebijuwa, A.S., Oyetola, S.O. and Akinola, J.O. (2012). Factors influencing high rate of commercial motorcycle accidents in Nigeria. *American International Journal of Contemporary Research*, *2*(11), 130-140.

[6] Norwegian Public Roads Administration. *Fatal motorcycle accidents 2005-2009*. Oslo: Directorate of Public Roads, 2011.

[7] Molinero, A., Perandones, J.M., Pedrero, D., Mansilla, A. and Martin, O. "Determination of accident causation and risk factors in traffic accidents from the point of view of motorcyclist users", in *3rd International Symposium on Accident Research*, Hannover – Germany, August 2012, pp. 139-148.

[8] Transportation Research Board. *Modeling operating speed: Synthesis report.* Washington D.C.: Transportation Research Circular, 2011.

[9] Dinh, D. and Kubota, H. (2013). Profile-speed data-based models to estimate operating speeds for urban residential streets with a 30 km/h speed limit, *International Association of Traffic and Safety Sciences Research*, *36*(2), 115-122.

[10] Fitzsimmons, E.J. *Development and analysis of vehicle trajectories and speed profiles along horizontal curves.* Iowa State University – Department of Civil, Construction, and Environmental Engineering, USA, 2011.

[11] Jun, J., Ogle, J. and Guensler, R. (2007). Relationships between crash involvement and temporal-spatial driving behavior activity patterns: Use of data for vehicles with global positioning systems. *Transportation Research Record: Journal of the Transportation Research Board, 2019*, 246-255.

[12] Jun, J., Guensler, R. and Ogle, J. "Potential GPS-Observed driving behavior exposure metrics for crash risk analysis", in *Transportation Research Board 93rd Annual Meeting*. Washington D.C., January 2014, 12p.

[13] Profillidis V., Eliou, N. and Botzoris, G. (2008).Utilisation des techniques GPS pour évaluer la perception du danger routier par le conducteur. *Transports*, *451*, 304-309.

[14] Lemonakis, P., Eliou, N., Botzoris, G. and Karakasidis, T. (2013). Contribution to the investigation of motorcyclists' speed prediction equations for two-lane rural roads. *Journal of Transportation Technologies*, *3*(3), 204-213.

[15] Lemonakis, P., Eliou, N., Karakasidis, T. and Botzoris, G. (2014). A new methodology for approaching motorcycle riders' behavior at curved road sections. *European Transport Research Review*, *6*(3), 303-314.

[16] Pratico, F.G. and Giunta, M. "Operational and safety effects of two-lane roads alignment", in *4th International Symposium on Highway Geometric Design*, Transportation Research Board, Valencia – Spain, June 2010, 14p.

[17] Castro, M., Sánchez, J.F., Ardila, N. and Melo, J. "Speed models for highway consistency analysis: A Colombian case study" in *4th International Symposium on Highway Geometric Design*, Transportation Research Board, Valencia – Spain, June 2010, 15p.

[18] Eliou, N., Profillidis, V. and Botzoris, G. (2008). "Experimental monitoring of characteristics of risk perception by drivers and appropriate modelling with the use of the fuzzy method", in *10th International Conference on Application of Advanced Technologies in Transportation*, Athens – Greece, May 2008.

[19] Field Operational Test Support Action (FESTA). *Primer on experimental procedures*. http://www.its.leeds.ac.uk/festa/downloads/FESTA%20Experimental%20Procedures%20Deliverable%202.3.pdf.

[20] Yannis, G., Golias, J. and Papadimitriou, E. (2005). Driver age and vehicle engine size effects on fault and severity in young motorcyclists accidents. *Accident Analysis and Prevention*, *37*(2), 327-333.

[21] Laporte, S. and Espié, S. (2010). Understanding risk taking behaviour within the context of PTW riders: A report on rider diversity with regard to attitudes, perceptions and behavioural choices. Paris: Institut National de Recherché sur les Transports et leur Sécurité.

[22] Islam, N.M. and Seneviratne, P.N. (1994). Evaluation of design consistency of two-lane rural highways. *Institute of Transportation Engineers Journal*, *64*(2), 28-31.

[23] Voigt, A.P. and Krammes, R.A. "An operational and safety evaluation of alternative horizontal curve design approaches on rural two-lane highways" in *International Symposium on Highway Geometric Design*

Practices, Texas Transportation Institute, Boston – Massachusetts, August 1999, pp. 11, 1-8.

[24] Wooldridge, M., Fitzpatrick, K., Harwood, D., Potts, I., Elefteriadou, L. and Torbic, D. (2003).*Geometric design consistency on high-speed rural two-lane roadways*. Washington D.C.: National Cooperative Highway Research Program, Transportation Research Board.

[25] Tate, F. and Turner, S. (2007). Road geometry and drivers speed choice. *Road and Transport Research*, *16*(4), 53-64.

[26] Mazzella, A., Pinna, F. and Piras, C. "Geostatical approach for operating speed modelling on Italian roads", in *4th International Symposium on Highway Geometric Design*, Transportation Research Board, Valencia – Spain, June 2010, 14p.

[27] Wong, Y.D. and Nicholson, A. (1992). Driver behaviour at horizontal curves: Risk compensation and the margin of safety. *Accident Analysis and Prevention*, *24*(4), 425-436.

[28] Perco, P. (2008). Comparison between powered two wheeler and passenger car free-flow speeds in urban areas. *Transportation Research Record: Journal of the Transportation Research Board*, *2074*, 77-84.

[29] Faezi, S.F., Hamid, H. and Davoodi, S.R. (2011). Predicting speed model of horizontal curves on exclusive motorcycle lane. *Australian Journal of Basic Applied Sciences*, *5*(5), 590-598.

[30] Fildes, N.B., Leening, C.A. and Corrigan, M.J. (1989). Speed perception: Drivers' judgments of safety and speed on rural straight and curved roads and for different following distances. Canberra, Australia: Department of Transport.

[31] Othman, S., Thomson, R. and Lannér, G. (2010). Are driving and overtaking on right curves more dangerous than on left curves? *Annals of Advances in Automotive Medicine*, *54*, 253-264.

[32] Koorey, G., Page, S., Stewart, P., Gu, J., Ellis, A., Henderson, R. and Cenek, P. (2002). Curve advisory speeds in New Zealand. Wellington, New Zealand: Transfund New Zealand Research Center.

[33] Bennett, C.R. (1994). A speed prediction model for rural two-lane highways. Ph.D. Dissertation, University of Auckland – Department of Civil Engineering, New Zealand.

[34] Ayman, A.M. and Gandhi, S.G. (2008). Development of models for predicting speed on horizontal curves for two-lane rural highways. *The Arabian Journal for Science and Engineering*, *33*(2), 365-377.

[35] Charlton, S.G. and de Pont, J.J. *Curve speed management*. Wellington, New Zealand: Land Transport New Zealand, 2007.

[36] Zegeer, C., Stewart, R., Reinfurt, D., Council, F., Neuman, T., Hamilton, E., Miller, T. and Hunter, W. (1990). *Cost effective geometric improvements for safety upgrading of horizontal curves*. Wilmington, North Carolina: Highway Safety Research Center.

[37] Lewis-Evans, B. and Charlton, S.G. (2006). Explicit and implicit processes in behavioural adaptation to road width. *Accident Analysis and Prevention*, *38*(3), 610-617.

[38] Good, C.M. (1978). A review of empirical studies of driver-vehicle behavior on road curves. In: ARRB Group, *Road curve geometry and driver behaviour*. Melbourne: De Beers Industrial Diamond Division Pty, 75-92.

[39] Glennon, C.J. and Weaver, G.D. (1971). The relationship of vehicles paths to highway curve design. Arlington, Texas: Texas Transportation Institute.

[40] Felipe, E. and Navin, F. (1998). Automobiles on horizontal curves: Experiments and observations. *Transportation Research Record: Journal of the Transportation Research Board*, *1628*, 50-56.

[41] Wong, Y.D. and Nicholson, A. (1992). Driver behavior at horizontal curves. *Accident Analysis and Prevention*, *24*(4), 425-436.

[42] Fitzsimmons, E., Nambisan, S., Souleyrette, R. and Kvam V. (2013). Analyses of vehicle trajectories and speed profiles along horizontal curves. *Journal of Transportation Safety and Security*, *5*(3), 189-207.

[43] Gawron, J.V. and Ranney, T.A. (1990). Curve negotiation performance in a driving simulator as a function of curve geometry. *Applied Ergonomics*, *21*(1), 33-38.

[44] Cenek, P.D. and Davies, R.W. "Crash risk relationships for improved safety management of roads", in *Towards Sustainable Land Transport Conference*, Wellington – New Zealand, November 2004, 16p.

[45] Glennon, C.J., Neuman, R.T. and Leisch, J.E. (1985). *Safety and operational considerations for design of rural curves*. Evanston, Illinois: Federal Highway Administration.

[46] Arbeitsgruppe Verkehrssicherheit, Verkehrssicherheit nachts – Verkehrstechnische Verbesserungen an der Strassenanlage. Bern, Switzerland: Eidgenössisches Justiz- und Polizeidepartement, 1980.

[47] Bullock, R. *Least Squares Circle Fit*. www.dtcenter.org/met/users/docs/write-ups/circle-fit.pdf.

[48] Psarianos, B. and Kontaratos, M. (2000). *Design, study and operation of junctions* (in Greek). Athens: National Technical University Press.

[49] Hurt, H.H., Quellet, V.J. and Thom, R.D. (1981). *Motorcycle accident cause factors and identification of countermeasures*. Washington D.C.: US Department of Transportation.

[50] de Lapparent, M. (2006). Empirical Bayesian analysis of accident severity for motorcyclists in large French urban areas. *Accident Analysis and Prevention, 38*(2), 260-268.

[51] Crundall, D., Humphrey, K. and Clarke, D. (2008). Perception and appraisal of approaching motorcycles at junctions. *Transportation Research Part F: Traffic Psychology and Behaviour, 11*(3), 159-167.

[52] Clarke, D., Ward, P., Bartle, C. and Truman, W. (2004). In-depth study of motorcycle accidents. London: Department for Transport.

[53] National Highway Traffic Safety Administration (NHTSA). Fatal two-vehicle motorcycle crashes. Washington D.C.: US Department of Transportation, 2007.

[54] Williams, J.M. and Hoffmann, R.E. (1979). Motorcycle conspicuity and traffic accidents. *Accident Analysis and Prevention, 11*(3), 209-224.

[55] Williams, J.M. and Hoffmann, R.E. (1979). Conspicuity of motorcycles. *Human Factors, 21*(5), 619-626.

[56] Smith, I.D. (1975). *An investigation to determine whether the daytime usage of motorcycle headlights and tail-lights should be made compulsory in Western Australia*. Perth, Australia: Department of Motor Vehicles.

[57] Wulf, G., Hancock, P. A. and Rahimi, M. (1989). Motorcycle conspicuity: An evaluation and synthesis of influential factors. *Journal of Safety Research, 20*(4), 153-176.

[58] Norwegian Public Roads Administration. *Design and operation of roads and traffic systems*. Oslo: Directorate of Public Roads, 2004.

[59] Association des Constructeurs Européens de Motocycles (ACEM). *Guidelines for PTW-safer road design in Europe*. Brussels, Belgium: ACEM, 2006.

[60] Branas, C.C. and Knudson, M.M. (2001). Helmet use laws and motorcycle rider death rates. *Accident Analysis and Prevention, 33*(5), 641-648.

[61] Savolainen, P. and Mannering, F. (2007). Probabilistic models of motorcyclists' injury severities in single- and multi-vehicle crashes. *Accident Analysis and Prevention, 39*(5), 955-963.

[62] Ahmed, A., Sadullah, A.F.M. and Yahya, A.S. (2015). Field study on the behavior of right-turning vehicles in Malaysia and their contribution on the safety of unsignalized intersections. *Transportation Research Part*

F: Traffic Psychology and Behaviour, in press (http://dx.doi.org/10.1016/j.trf.2015.03.006).

[63] Pai, W.C. and Saleh, W. (2007). An analysis of motorcyclist injury severity under various traffic control measures at three-legged junctions in the UK. *Safety Science*, *45*(8), 832-847.

[64] Haworth, N. and Mulvihill, C. (2005). Review of motorcycle licensing and training. Melbourne, Australia: Monash University Accident Research Center.

In: Traffic Accidents and Safety: New Research ISBN: 978-1-63485-517-4
Editor: Garrett Bowman

Chapter 4

RISK AND PROTECTIVE FACTORS ASSOCIATED WITH MOTORCYCLE INJURY SEVERITY IN THE UNITED STATES

Deogratias Eustace * ***and Sunanda Dissanayake***
[1]Department of Civil and Environmental Engineering and Engineering Mechanics, University of Dayton, Dayton, OH, US
[2]Department of Civil Engineering, Kansas State University, Manhattan, KS, US

ABSTRACT

According to the Centers for Disease Control and Prevention, road crashes are one of the major causes of morbidity and mortality in the United States. The Healthy People 2020 has indicated that accidents are a major public health issue. Most motor-vehicle related events resulting in injury, disability, or death are predictable and preventable. Injuries are the leading cause of death for Americans aged 1 to 44 years and a leading cause of disability for all ages, regardless of sex, race/ethnicity, or socioeconomic status. Although motorcycles represent approximately 3% of all registered vehicles in the United States, motorcycling accounts for more than 13% of highway traffic fatalities. While fatalities normally represent a small percent of other motor vehicle occupants, fatalities can

* Department of Civil and Environmental Engineering and Engineering Mechanics, University of Dayton, 300 College Park, Dayton, OH 45469-0243. Email: deo.eustace@udayton.edu.

be as high as 40% for the motorcyclists when involved in accidents (or traffic crashes as typically referred to by transportation safety professionals). Motorcyclists are more vulnerable in crashes due to their lack of protection like enclosed vehicles do to motor vehicle occupants, so they are more likely to be severely injured or killed. Therefore, there is a motivation among stakeholders to decrease the injury severity of motorcyclists. A clear understanding of the factors influencing injury severity levels due to motorcycle crashes and the related evidence prevention strategies is of paramount importance. When examining a topic of motorcycle injury severity, it is important to keep into consideration of different issues that include the definition and concept of injury severity, trends in motorcycle crashes, motorcycle-related policies and laws, knowledge of risk and protective factors. The main purpose of this chapter is to discuss the risk factors and protective factors related to injury severity of motorcycle crashes in the US. Important aspects related to motorcycle crashes' injury severity such as methodological challenges related to conceptual clarity and measurement are discussed. In addition, implications for education, research, practice and policy including laws and enforcement are highlighted so that the overall motorcycle safety situation could be improved.

Keywords: motorcycle, motorcycle rider, motorcyclist, crash severity

INTRODUCTION

Motorcycle crashes tend to lead into more severe injuries and fatalities than crashes that involve other types of motor vehicles. Although motorcycles represent approximately 3% of all registered vehicles in the United States, motorcycling accounts for more than 13% of highway traffic fatalities. While fatalities normally represent a small percent of other motor vehicle occupants, fatalities can be as high as 40% for the motorcyclists when involved in traffic crashes. Motorcyclists are more vulnerable in crashes due to their lack of protection like enclosed vehicles do to motor vehicle occupants, so they are more likely to be severely injured or killed. Therefore, there is a motivation among stakeholders to decrease the injury severity of motorcyclists. A clear understanding of the factors influencing injury severity levels due to motorcycle crashes and the related evidence prevention strategies is of paramount importance. This chapter discusses the risk factors and protective factors related to injury severity of motorcycle crashes in the United States. Important aspects related to motorcycle crashes' injury severity such as methodological challenges related to conceptual clarity and measurement are discussed.

According to Pickrell and Starnes (2008), the following definitions of the terminologies pertaining to motorcycle users, based on definitions used by the National Highway Traffic Safety Administration (NHTSA) need to be clarified:

- *A motorcycle rider* is the person operating or in control of the motorcycle.
- *A motorcycle passenger* is the person seated behind the rider and not in control of the motorcycle.
- *A motorcyclist* is a collective term used for any combined reference to the rider and passenger of the motorcycle.

Definition and Concept of Injury Severity

In addition to reducing the number of crashes involving motorcycles, reducing injury severities associated with those crashes is one of the most important aspects of promoting motor cycle safety. Progress in promoting safety could be evaluated by considering reductions in injury severity levels experienced by those involved in motorcycle crashes. It is therefore important to properly define injury severities so that the evaluations could be done in a meaningful manner.

Typically, injury severity is recorded discretely using a five point scale, which is often referred to as the KABCO scale. The categories include:

- Fatal injury or killed (K),
- Incapacitating injury (A),
- Non-incapacitating injury (B),
- Possible injury (C), and
- Property damage only (O).

In safety studies related to transportation engineering literature this five point scale is commonly used. However there are other types of injury severity data that include detailed information on trauma location and extent of injury which may be a combination of discrete and continuous variables. Abbreviated Injury Scale (AIS) which was originally developed by the American

Association for Automotive Medicine, the Organ Injury Scales (OIS) proposed by the American Association for the Surgery of Trauma and the Injury Severity Score (ISS) used by hospitals are some of the examples of methods of accounting for injury severity.

Many electronic databases used by various states or very popular databases at national level such as the Fatality Analysis Reporting System (FARS) or General Estimates System (GES), use traditional discrete data forms, mainly based on police-reported data. These data provide crash detail information. The crash related records include crash severity, vehicle in error, date of crash, time of crash, crash location, type of road, alcohol-related, drug related, speed related, etc.; records for each unit involved in the crash include unit type (e.g., motor vehicle, motorcycle, bicycle, pedestrian, etc.), point of impact, number of occupants, etc.; and records for each person involved in the crash such as type of person (e.g., driver, occupant, pedestrian), injury severity, age, gender, safety equipment used, etc.).

MOTORCYCLE CRASH TYPES AND TRENDS

There are more than 8 million motorcycles registered in the United States over the last several years and the number and rate of motorcycle crashes are fluctuating even though slight improvements could be seen in the overall trend. Still, in 2013, there were 4,668 motorcyclists killed in motor vehicle traffic crashes and there were an estimated 88,000 motorcyclists injured during 2013 (NCSA, 2015). Table 1 shows the variation of Motorcycle crash numbers and rates in the recent years.

Data shows that in 2013 the most harmful event for 2,448 (51%) of the 4,774 motorcycles involved in fatal crashes was a collision with a motor vehicle in transport. (NCSA, 2015) In two-vehicle crashes, 74% of the motorcycles involved in motor vehicle traffic crashes were frontal collisions. Only 6% were struck in the rear.

Motorcycles are more frequently involved in fatal collisions with fixed objects than other vehicles. In 2013, 22% of the motorcycles involved in fatal crashes collided with fixed objects, compared to 18% for passenger cars, 14% for light trucks, and 4% for large trucks.

Table 1. Motorcyclists Killed and Injured, and Fatality and Injury Rates, 2005–2013 (Source: NCSA, 2015)

Year	Killed	Registered Vehicles	Fatality Rate*	Vehicle Miles Traveled (millions)	Fatality Rate**
2005	4,576	6,227,146	73.48	10,454	43.77
2006	4,837	6,678,958	72.42	12,049	40.14
2007	5,174	7,138,476	72.48	21,396	24.18
2008	5,312	7,752,926	68.52	20,811	25.52
2009	4,469	7,929,724	56.36	20,822	21.46
2010	4,518	8,009,503	56.41	18,513	24.40
2011	4,630	8,437,502	54.87	18,542	24.97
2012	4,986	8,454,939	58.97	21,385	23.32
2013	4,668	8,404,687	55.54	20,366	22.92
Year	Injured	Registered Vehicles	Injury Rate*	Vehicle Miles Traveled (millions)	Injury Rate**
2005	87,000	6,227,146	1,402	10,454	835
2006	88,000	6,678,958	1,312	12,049	727
2007	103,000	7,138,476	1,443	21,396	481
2008	96,000	7,752,926	1,238	20,811	461
2009	90,000	7,929,724	1,130	20,822	430
2010	82,000	8,009,503	1,024	18,513	443
2011	81,000	8,437,502	965	18,542	439
2012	93,000	8,454,939	1,099	21,385	434
2013	88,000	8,404,687	1,052	20,366	434

* Rate per 100,000 registered vehicles **Rate per 100 million vehicle miles traveled.

In 2013, there were 2,182 two-vehicle fatal crashes involving a motorcycle and another type of vehicle. In 42% (922) of these crashes, the other vehicles were turning left while the motorcycles were going straight, passing, or overtaking other vehicles. Both vehicles were going straight in 456 crashes (21%) (NCSA, 2015).

Motorcycle Helmet Laws and Their Effectiveness

One area in need of immediate attention in terms of motorcycle safety is the use of helmets. Motorcycle helmet laws in the United States vary significantly among the states. As of 2016, there are 19 states and District of Colombia with universal (mandatory) helmet laws, 27 states with partial helmet laws and three states with no helmet laws at all, as shown in Figure 1 (IIHS, 2016).

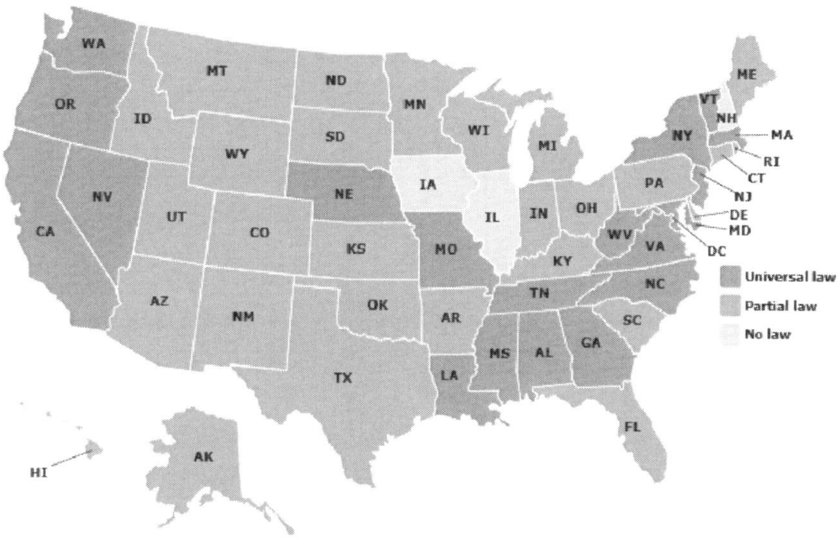

Figure 1. Motorcycle Laws in the United States (Source: IIHS, 2016).

Motorcycle safety-related studies in the past have addressed helmet use, helmet-use laws in different states, effects of helmet use on motorcycle crash outcomes, factors related to motorcycle fatalities, and injuries, using a variety of databases, some of which are summarized here.

Branas and Knudson (2001) investigated motorcycle rider fatality rates between states with mandatory motorcycle helmet laws and those without the laws. Competing influences of variables such as population density, weather conditions, alcohol consumption, maximum speed limit, urban vs. rural roads, motorcycle engine size, and age of the motorcycle riders were analyzed on the fatality rates of motorcyclists. Bivariate analyses demonstrated that states with motorcycle helmet laws have significantly higher fatality rates per 10,000 registered motorcycles compared to states without helmet laws. After simultaneously adjusting for other factors using multivariate regression models, fatality rates in states with mandatory motorcycle helmet laws were shown to be lower than those of states without helmet laws.

Peek-Asa et al. (1999) examined the prevalence of non-standard helmet use among motorcycle riders following introduction of a mandatory helmet law and the prevalence of head injuries among a sample of non-standard helmet users involved in motorcycle crashes. Among the injured riders examined in 1992, exactly one-third, whose crash reports indicated non-standard helmet use, had 15.5% fatalities of non-helmeted riders compared to 13.6% of helmeted riders. Among the riders wearing non-standard helmets, 75% sustained head injuries of any severity which was significantly greater than riders not wearing a helmet, of which 51.9% had any injuries. Average head injury severity for riders identified as wearing non-standard helmets was 82.65, which was significantly higher than 1.56 for riders not wearing helmets and 0.96 for riders wearing standard helmets.

Results of surveys conducted by Williams et al. (1979) indicate that when helmet use is legally required of all motorcyclists, nearly 100% wear helmets. Helmet-use rates were substantially lower when use is not required of any motorcyclists, or when helmet-use laws covering all motorcyclists are amended so that only those under age of 18 years are covered. Amending helmet-use laws so that only young motorcyclists are required to wear helmets appears to have little impact on user rates. Based on the study completed in 1979, overall helmet use rate in New Orleans, Louisiana; Phoenix, Arizona; and Texas, where such laws existed, was 48%, similar to the use rate in Los Angeles, California (46%), where such helmet use was not required of any motorcyclists at the time.

An analysis by Mayrose (2008) show that from 1995–2003, mandatory helmet law states had a 22.3% rise in total fatalities, with a 3% increase in helmet use among fatally injured riders in these states. Partial-law states had a 32.9% increase in total motorcycle fatalities with a 1.2% increase in helmet use, while the three other states with no helmet law at all had a 21.78% increase in total motorcycle fatalities with only a 2% increase in helmet use. The increase in fatalities can be attributed to an increased number of motorcyclists on the road over this time period. It was found that motorcyclists are more likely to wear helmets in states with mandatory helmet laws than their counterparts in states with only partial helmet laws or no laws at all.

Rutledge et al. (1993) studied the association of helmet use with the outcome of motorcycle crashes, controlling for severity of the crash as measured by a modified injury severity score that excluded head injury. Risk of head injuries was found to be nearly twice as high in unhelmeted riders. This study illustrated the increased likelihood of head injury when a helmet is not worn, but also showed helmet use is not a significant factor determining morbidity rates, hospital charges, and length of stay. There were, however, some unanticipated findings in the study. There were no significant differences in overall mortality, mean trauma scores, mean hospital stays, mean hospital charges, or percentage of cases discharged to rehabilitation facilities between helmeted and unhelmeted patients.

Wilson (1990) found that although effectiveness of helmet use depends on many factors (e.g., driver age, speed, crash direction), but in assessing effectiveness, motorcycle helmets are estimated to be 29% effective in preventing motorcycle rider fatalities. Further, although motorcycle helmets saved an estimated 670 lives in 1987, they could have prevented an additional 693 fatalities if 100% of motorcycle riders wore helmets. In examining the data, it was evident there is a consistency in helmet usage patterns between the rider and the passenger, such that when the rider is helmeted so tends to be the passenger. This is also true when the rider is unhelmeted.

In a recent study by Dissanayake and Shaheed (2012) state-level motorcycle rider fatality rates were investigated while considering various factors, including helmet laws, using the generalized least-squares (GLS) regression modeling of statewide rider fatality rates utilizing data from all 50 states and the District of Columbia.. The intention was to develop statistical models to predict state-level motorcycle safety parameters while taking various factors into account. From the GLS modeling carried out in that study, a statistically significant relationship was found between helmet laws and motorcyclist fatalities per 10,000 registered motorcycles and per 100,000 populations in a state. Specifically, that study showed that states with mandatory helmet laws had 5.6% fewer motorcycle fatalities per 10,000 registrations and 7.85% fewer motorcycle fatalities per 100,000 population.

Risk and Protective Factors Related to Injury Severity of Motorcycle Crashes

Numerous studies have been conducted over the years and several factors have been consistently identified as contributing to motorcycle injury severity in the United States. Therefore, this section discusses some of the risk and protective factors that have been widely acknowledged. Based on the published literature and annual crash records in the United States, motorcycle riding continues being a risky endeavor, for example in 2013 motorcyclists were estimated to be 26 times more likely to to be killed and 5 times more likely to be injured when compared to passenger car occupants per mile traveled (NCSA, 2015; IIHS, 2016).

Alcohol use is one of the most highly cited risk factors for drivers of all types of vehicles but more worse for motorcycle riders. In the United States alcohol-impaired is defined as a motor vehicle driver or motorcycle rider with blood alcohol concentration (BACs) of 0.08 grams per deciliter (g/dL) or higher (NCSA, 2015). The percentage of motorcycle riders involved in fatal crashes with BACs of at least 0.08 grams per deciliter (legally alcohol-impaired) is typically higher than any other type of motor vehicle drivers (Peek-Asa et al. 1999; NCSA, 2008; Soderstorm et al. 1993, NCSA, 2015). For example in 2013, 27% of motorcycle operators who were involved in fatal crashes had a BAC above 0.08, 23% for passenger car drivers, 21% for light-truck drivers and only 2% for large truck drivers (NCSA, 2015).

Helmet use is another important factor in relation to injury severity of motorcyclists. An extensive study by Branas and Knudson (2001) found that motorcycle rider death rates in states with universal (mandatory) helmet use laws were lower on average than death rates in states with non-universal helmet use laws. Pickrell and Starnes (2008) comment that in the same crash event, an un-helmeted motorcyclist is about 40% more likely to suffer a fatal head injury and 15% more likely to suffer a nonfatal injury when compared with a helmeted motorcyclist. The National Center for Statistics and Analysis estimates that helmets are effective in preventing the likelihood of fatality by 37% for motorcycle riders and 41% for motorcycle passengers (NCSA, 2015). The Insurance Institute for Highway Safety (IIHS) argues that a helmet is the most important piece of motorcycle safety equipment (IIHS, 2016). Helmets decrease the severity of head injuries and the likelihood of death and NHTSA estimates that motorcycle riders who don't wear helmet are 3 times more likely than those who wear helmet to sustain traumatic brain injuries in the event of a crash (IIHS, 2016). Gielen and Samuels (2012) report that helmets are estimated to reduce the risk of head injury by 69%, death by 42%, and therefore associated with reductions in overall injury severity and likelihood of needing of hospitalization. Additional studies whose findings agree that non-helmet use increases odds of higher injury severity levels include Lardelli-Claret et al. (2005), Chang and Yeh (2006), Lin and Kraus (2009), Eustace et al., (2010), Shaheed and Dissanayake, (2011), Fagnant and Kockelman, (2015), etc.

According to the IIHS some kinds of motorcycles are riskier than others (IIHS, 2016). *Supersport bikes are* another factor that has been associated with high motorcycle fatalities. These motorcycles are built on a racing platform and typically have more horsepower per pound (powerful) and very fast but they are cheap and affordable and thus attractive and popular with young riders who are looking for fun (speeding) and daring and hence prone to higher risk driving behaviors (IIHS, 2007; III, 2016). Driver death for supersport motorcycles are estimated to be four times higher than those of cruiser/standard motorcycles (Teoh and Campbell, 2010; III, 2016; IIHS, 2016). In addition, among fatally injured motorcycle riders, the riders of supersport motorcycles happen to be the youngest, with an average age of 27 while touring motorcycle riders tend to be the oldest at 51 years old (IIHS, 2016; III, 2016).

The other risk factor that has been linked with severe injury and fatalities for motorcycle riders involves *unlicensed or improperly licensed riders and riders with previous driving convictions*. According to NHTSA (NCSA, 2015) a valid motorcycle license comprises a rider having a valid driver license (non-CDL license status) with a motorcycle endorsement or motorcycle-only license. Before riding on public highways in all fifty states and the District of Columbia motorcycle riders are required to obtain a motorcycle operator license or endorsement. However, many motorcycle riders are not properly licensed (III, 2016). In 2013, while 25% of motorcycle riders involved in fatal crashes did not have a valid motorcycle license but only 13% of drivers of passenger vehicles involved in fatal crashes did not have valid licenses (NCSA, 2015). Furthermore, motorcycle riders tend to have the highest percentage of drivers with previous driving convictions such as driving impaired, speeding and revocation when compared with drivers of other vehicle types (NCSA, 2015). For example, in 2013 riders involved in fatal crashes were 1.2 more likely to have received previous license suspensions or revocations when compared with passenger vehicle drivers (NCSA, 2015).

Speeding is another major perennial risk factor normally related to severe traffic injury severity levels. Once again, motorcycle riders are typically more likely to be involved in speeding-related fatal crashes than other drivers. For instance, NHTSA reports that in 2013 the percent of motorcycle riders involved in fatal crashes that were speeding-related was 34% compared to 21% for drivers of passenger cars, 18% for light truck drivers and 8% for large truck drivers (NCSA, 2015). Accordingly, a number of previous research studies agree on the association of motorcycle speeding with increased injury and crash severity levels (e.g., Shankar and Mannering 1996; Clarke et al. 2004; Lardelli-Claret et al. 2005; Shankar and Varghese 2006, Chimba and Sando 2010, Eustace et al., 2010), etc.

Some research studies have shown that *population density* generally affects highway mortality rates but specifically correlates more with motorcycle rider fatalities. Usually, when the population density increases, it leads into frequent stops on the highways and streets as compared to lower population density areas where drivers can drive with fewer interruptions (Keeler 1994; Calkins and Zlatoper 2001; Cohen and Einav 2003; Farmer and Williams 2005). A study by Branas and Knudson (2001) reports a significant positive relationship between state-level population densities and motorcycle rider death rates.

Weather condition has also been found to correlate with motorcycle fatal crashes. Weather as measured in terms of annual daily mean temperature and annual precipitation, is correlated with motorcycle riders' fatality rates. While the association of temperature to motorcycle fatality rates is highly positive, precipitation's association with motorcycle riders' fatality rates is negatively related (Branas and Knudson, 2001; Houston and Richardson, 2008). Based on their findings, Branas and Knudson (2001) argue that these two factors likely affect the length of the riding season (and hence exposure to crashes) in each state in the United States. For example, states with higher annual daily temperatures and lower annual precipitation (e.g., southwestern states) have relatively longer riding seasons and therefore greater chances for motorcycle fatalities to occur whereas states with lower annual daily temperatures and higher annual precipitation (e.g., northeastern states) have relatively shorter riding seasons and fewer motorcycle fatalities (Branas and Knudson, 2001).

In addition, a study by Morris (2006) reports that the largest percentages of motorcyclist fatalities and injuries occur during warm months associated with the smallest percentages of normalized heating degree days and the largest percentages of precipitation inches. On the other hand, the smallest percentages of fatalities and injuries occur during cold months associated with the largest percentages of normalized heating degree days and the smallest percentages of precipitation inches.

Higher *levels of education* have been considered as a factor in promoting personal healthy behaviors (Grossman, 1975). Generally, healthy behaviors have been associated with compliance with existing laws such as wearing motorcycle helmets, wearing seat belts, obeying traffic rules, etc. (Dissanayake and Shaheed, 2012) Several studies show that education is negatively associated with motor vehicle fatality rates (e.g., Calkins and Zlatoper, 2001; Braver, 2003; Muelleman et al., 1992). According to Paulozzi (2005), income is usually postulated to be negatively correlated with traffic fatalities because wealthy people are generally regarded as more aware and place a higher value on safety, and possess the means to enhance it. Nevertheless, in the case of motorcycle riders, income per capita has been found to be positively correlated with higher motorcycle fatalities (Houston and Richardson, 2008). Houston and Richardson (2008) argue that since motorcycles are expensive and luxurious, in the United States they are more often used as recreational vehicles rather than a primary mode of transportation and hence affluent people are the most likely to buy and ride motorcycles as extra luxurious recreational vehicles.

Motorcycle training is an important factor in reducing motorcycle-related crashes. Riding a motorcycle requires additional mental and physical skills than those needed in driving motor vehicles (IIHS, 2016) and motorcycle riders are more vulnerable road users when compared with drivers of other vehicle types due to their lack of protection when involved in a crash (Rifaat et al., 2012). A study by Fagnant and Kockelman (2015) suggests that motorcycle riders who have received motorcycle training are less likely to have been involved in a motorcycle crash at some point in their riding history. That is why motorcycle riders are always recommended to attend periodic training in order to increase their awareness of traffic safety, improve on their defensive motorcycle maneuvers and increase their odds of avoiding traffic crashes and severe injuries.

According to Fagnant and Kockelman (2015) top riders recommend to other motorcycle riders that protective factors of injury severity include wearing a helmet, avoiding riding under the influence (of alcohol or drugs), and to obtain motorcycle training. Additionally, riding a motorcycle equipped with antilock brakes and avoiding driving a motorcycle at excessive speed constitute additional protective factors of motorcycle injury severity. Furthermore, the results from the study by Fagnant and Kockeleman (2015) suggest that inexperienced riders on long-distance trips, students and riders with criminal convictions are at greater risk of being involved in motorcycle crashes than other riders.

According to IIHS (2016) an *antilock braking system (ABS)* reduces the risk of a motorcycle crash. ABS prevents wheels from locking up, which is an absolutely essential feature for a motorcycle. While for a motor vehicle a wheel lockup might simply result into a skid, for a motorcycle, it often results into a serious fall and hence severe injuries and the Insurance Institute for Highway Safety estimates that the rate of fatal crashes is 31% lower for motorcycles equipped with optional antilock brakes when compared with similar models without them (IIHS, 2016).

Motorcycle conspicuity is another important factor in motorcycle safety. Wells et al. (2004) show that low motorcycle rider conspicuity may increase the risk of motorcycle crash related injury. A study by Shaeed et al. (2012) shows that leading motorcycles with riders having bright yellow clothing and helmet were detected at the greatest distance, which may enhance the motorcyclists' safety. The US crash data for 2013 show that the most harmful event for 51% of motorcycles involved in fatal crashes was a collision with a motor vehicle in transport (NCSA, 2015); also in 42% of two-vehicle fatal crashes involving a motorcycle and another type of vehicle, the other vehicles were turning left while the motorcycles were going straight, passing, or overtaking other vehicles. These types of crashes can be partly contributed due to the inability of a motor vehicle driver to see the motorcycle or low motorcycle conspicuity (Shaheed et al., 2013). Protective factors for motorcyclists include the increased use of reflective or fluorescence clothing, white or light colored helmets, and daytime headlights (Wells et al., 2004; Shaheed et al., 2012).

Other risk factors as related to motorcycle injury severity include road *bends (curves)* and *grades*, which had been found to have substantial affects in the motorcyclist's fatality and incapacitating injury rates. Studies have shown that curved and graded segments have higher motorcyclist fatality rate when compared with level and straight road segments (e.g., Elliott et al., 2003; Chimba and Sando, 2010; Eustace et al., 2010). In addition, *nighttime* crashes and/or crashes in *dark lighting* conditions tend to result into a higher than average fatality rates (Eustace et al., 2010; Shaheed and Dissanayake, 2011; Dissanayake and Shaheed, 2012; NCSA, 2015).

Methodological Challenges Related to Conceptual Clarity and Measurement

Over the years, researchers have attempted to relate various factors (independent variables) to motorcycle crash or injury severity (dependent variable). In order to understand risk factors that increase the likelihood of injury severity in motorcycle crashes, various modeling techniques have been used by researchers. Statistical methods that have been commonly used by researchers in analyzing factors affecting motorcycle crash-related injury severity include: log-linear models (e.g., Haque et al., 2012); ordered logit (ologit) and ordered probit (oprobit) models (e.g., O'Donnell and Connor, 1996; Quddus et al.,. 2002; Rifaat et al., 2012); multinomial logit (MNL) models (e.g., Shankar and Mannering, 1996; Savolainen and Mannering, 2007; Jones et al., 2013); multinomial probit (MNP) models (e.g., Chimba and Sando, 2010; Eustace et al., 2010); nested logit (nlogit) models (e.g.,

Savolainen and Mannering, 2007), mixed logit (mlogit) models (e.g., Pai et al., 2009; Shaheed et al., 2013), etc.

Shanker and Mannering (1996) used a multinomial logit (MNL) model in analyzing single-vehicle motorcycle crash severity using data from the state of Washington. Savolainen and Mannering (2007) used nested logit (nlogit) and multinomial (MNL) models in analyzing injury severities of single-and multi-vehicle crashes employing crash data from Indiana. Chimba and Sando (2010) used multinomial logit (MNL) and multinomial probit (MNP) models in assessing motorcycle injury severities using data from Florida. Eustace et al. (2010) used a multinomial probit model (MNP) when analyzing risk factors associated with motorcycle-related fatalities in Ohio. Shaheed and Dissanayake (2011) utilized a logistic regression model in studying risk factors associated with motorcycle crash severity in Kansas. Shaheed et al. (2013) used a mixed logit (mlogit) model to examine two-vehicle crash severities involving a motorcycle utilizing data from Iowa. Jones et al. (2013) investigated factors influencing the severity of crashes caused by motorcyclists in Alabama by using a multinomial logit (MNL) model. Based on the foregoing discussion, it is obvious that a variety of methods have been selected and utilized by researchers.

Lin and Kraus (2008) point out that some inconsistent results have been observed on the relationship of universal helmet laws and motorcycle deaths and can be partly attributed to the differences in the analytical models utilized. Compared with other models, Lin and Kraus (2008) also suggest that when more than two levels of motorcycle injuries are the outcome variable, proportional odds models (such as ordered logit and ordered probit models) in which the correlation of multiple crashes involving the same individual is adjusted for by the generalized estimating equation (GEE) are more appropriate.

By far, the ordered logit (ologit) and multinomial (MNL) models have been the most popular choices in the analysis of crash and injury severity data (Savolainen et al., 2011). Each analysis method used has its strengths and weaknesses, which need to be identified and known with regard to the type of data to be analyzed and the assumptions underlying a particular method. It is widely believed that crash severity and injury severity as dependent variables are typical ordinal variables (e.g., Lin and Kraus, 2008; Wang and Abdel-Aty, 2008; Eustace et al., 2010; Savolainen et al., 2011). An ordinal variable is the one where the order matters but not the difference between the values. For example, injury levels defined as non-incapacitating injury, incapacitating injury, and fatal injury, these present three levels with increasing order of injury severity but you can't determine the difference between them. However, according to Savolainen and Mannering (2007) one potential problem with ordered probability models in determining injury severity levels underlies with the police officers' underreporting of non-injury crashes. This may result in biased and inconsistent model coefficient estimates. Another potential problem is the restrictive nature of parallel lines (same slope) assumption of ordered models, which restricts the slope to be the same value for all outcome levels (Long 1997; Park 2009, Williams, 2006, Mergia et al., 2013).

Most of the reviewed publications do not explain how this condition was met or if the condition was tested. Due to this problem with ordered logit models, some researchers recommend the use of unordered multinomial models in evaluating the effects of variables in each injury severity because they do not impose restrictive conditions typical of ordered logit models (Savolainen and Mannering 2007). For these kinds of models, besides losing the ability to account for the ordinal nature of injury data (i.e., ordering of injury-severity outcomes), however, multinomial logit models are principally susceptible to correlation of unobserved effects from one injury-severity level to the next, which lead into violation of the model's independence of irrelevant alternatives (IIA) property (Chimba and Sando, 2010; Eustace et al., 2010; Savolainen et al., 2011).

Hujer (2010) suggests that two ways of avoiding the IIA errors include the use of nested logit models or the use of multinomial probit models. In addition, the mixed logit models have been suggested for the same reasons (Pai et al. 2009; Malyshkina and Mannering 2010). Another method, which is recommended, capable of overcoming problems of both ordered logit and multinomial logit models is the use of the generalized ordered logit (gologit) models, which are capable of relaxing the restrictive nature of conventional ordered logit models and at the same time keeping the ordered nature of injury severity variables (Williams, 2006; Wang and Abdel-Aty, 2008; Wang et al., 2009; Mergia et al., 2013).

Implications for Education, Research, Practice and Policy

Safer motorcycle riding, which translates into reducing the number of motorcyclists' crashes and their injury severity should involve key stakeholders working together to integrate and leverage the 3'E's of traffic safety, i.e., Engineering, Enforcement and Education into one context to maximize key resources. These should be activities that will reduce motorcyclist injury severity risk factors or in other words, increasing or enhancing the protective factors.

Implications for Education

Some risk factors contributing to motorcycle severe injuries can be counter-measured through educational and enforcement strategies. This aspect should implement various issues including the following:

- Enhance and expand current motorcycle training and outreach programs to reach all motorcycle operators, motor vehicle drivers and transportation professionals in order to improve motorcycle safety throughout the nation. Emphasis should highly target novice riders and refresher training programs for experienced riders especially those who can be identified as potential risk riders.
- Since low physical conspicuity is believed to be one of the contributing factors in a substantial percentage of motorcycle injury-causing crashes, there is a need to institute laws requiring daytime use of headlights and encouraging measures that enhance better visibility of motorcycle riders on the road such as wearing retroreflective clothing and helmets.
- Alcohol/drugs use and excessive speeding are two persistently major concerns of traffic safety. Educational campaigns and enforcement campaigns with high visibility should be expanded and continued throughout the country with an increased stress to both motorcycle and motor vehicle drivers on the awareness of the effects of speeding, alcohol/drugs impairment, careful driving on road bends and vertical grades.
- It is recommended to use a combination of educational efforts such as media, advertisement boards, licensing bureaus, and motorcycle riders' organizations and clubs.

Implications for Research

While efforts to implement countermeasure strategies designed to reduce motorcycle crash-related injuries and fatalities in the auspices of education, enforcement, and engineering are on the continuous basis, correspondingly research efforts on behavioral safety, motorcycle safety technology, etc., should continue. Research efforts should be designed to build on what we know and learn today and expand our knowledge of motorcycle injury severity and improved safety performance for future implementation into existing programs.

Implications for Policy

From our review of the literature several implications for policy concerning reducing motorcycle injury severity in the United States should include some of the following:

- Encourage all states to adopt stronger helmet use laws by enacting universal helmet use laws that protect all motorcyclists. Maintain and enforce all-rider helmet use laws. In addition, local enforcement officers should help their states and local jurisdictions in making sure that they are effectively enforcing all rider helmet use laws and other laws that pertain to traffic safety.
- Make sure all states' motor vehicle licensing bureaus or agencies are promoting and requiring motorcycle operator licensure or endorsement for anybody who purchases, registers and/or rides a motorcycle.
- Promote the installation of antilock braking systems (ABS) to all motorcycles sold in the United States as records show that motorcycles with ABS reduce the likelihood of motorcycle-related fatalities per registered motorcycle compared to identical models not equipped with ABS.
- States and other responsible agencies should ensure motorcycle helmets sold in all states meet federal standards.
- Encourage all states to pass a law that requires all motorcycles to have headlights on all of the time in order to improve motorcycle conspicuousness and also encourage wearing protective clothing and

other polices that will enhance and improve motorcyclists' visibility on the road.

Implications for Practice

Implications for practice may target engineering solutions as a component of 3 E's of traffic safety with regard to reducing injury severity related to motorcycle. This aspect should aim at improving and retrofitting existing transportation infrastructure and incorporating in safety features when designing new transportation infrastructure. Engineering measures may include:

- Responsible jurisdictions should identify and develop solutions for known locations prone to motorcycle crashes.
- Conduct road safety audits in order to qualitatively estimate and report on potential road safety issues and hence identify opportunities for safety improvements for all road users
- Make roads resistant to skidding and provide advance-warning signs especially designed to target and alert motorcycle riders.

CONCLUSION

This chapter discussed important issues pertaining to motorcycle crash related injury severity in the United States. Issues related to trends and type of motorcycle crashes, helmet use laws and their effectiveness in reducing severe injuries and deaths; the risk and protective factors related to motorcycle injury severity in the United States were discussed. In addition, methodological challenges related to evaluating factors affecting motorcycle injury severity were highlighted, and finally implications for education, research, practice and policy including laws and enforcement were briefly introduced so that the overall motorcycle safety situation could be improved.

REFERENCES

Branas, C. C. and Knudson, M. M., (2001). Helmet laws and motorcycle rider fatality rates. *Accident Analysis and Prevention, 33*(5), 641–648.

Braver, E. R. R. (2003). Hispanic origin and socioeconomic status in relation to motor vehicle occupant fatality rates and risk factors among adults. *Accident Analysis and Prevention, 35*, 295–309.

Calkins, L. N. and Zlatoper, T. J. (2001). The effects of mandatory seat belt laws on motor vehicle fatalities in the United States. *Social Science Quarterly, 82*, 133–139.

Chang, H. and Yeh, T. (2006). Risk factors to driver fatalities in single-vehicle crashes: comparisons between non-motorcycle drivers and motorcyclists. *Journal of Transportation Engineering, 132*, 227-236.

Chimba, D. and Sando, T. (2010). Multinomial probability assessment of motorcycle injury severity. *Advances in Transportation. Studies, an International Journal, 20*, 2010, 73-80.

Clarke, D. D., Ward, P., Bartle, C. and Truman, W. (2004). *In-depth study of motorcycle accidents* (No. 54, p. 67). Road safety research report. Department for Transport, London, UK.

Cohen, A. and Einav, L. (2003). The effects of mandatory seat belt laws on driving behavior and traffic fatalities. *The Review of Economics and Statistics, 85*, 828–843.

Dissanayake and Shaheed. (2012). *Evaluation of motorcycle safety in Kansas*. Final Report No. K-TRAN: KSU-09-1. Topeka, KS: Kansas Department of Transportation.

Elliott, M.A., Baughan, C. J., Broughton, J., Chinn, B., Grayson, G. B., Knowles, J., Smith, L. R. and Simpson, H. (2003). *Motorcycle safety: a scoping study*. Crowthorne, England: TRL Limited.

Eustace, D., Indupuru, V. K. and Hovey, P. (2010). Identification of risk factors associated with motorcycle-related fatalities in Ohio. *Journal of Transportation Engineering, 137*(7), 474-480.

Farmer, C. M. and Williams, A. F. (2005). Effect on fatality risk of changing from secondary to primary seat belt enforcement. *Journal of Safety Research, 36*, 189–194.

Fagnant, D.J. and Kockelman, K.M. (2015). U.S. motorcycle use: crash experiences, safety perspectives, and countermeasures. *Journal of Transportation Safety and Security, 7* (1), 20-39.

Gielen, A. and Samuels, A. (2012). Preventing injuries: a resource for state policy makers. Retrieved from http://www.jhsph.edu/research/centers-and-institutes/johns-hopkins-center-for-injury-research-and-policy/publications_resources/CenterPubs/PolicyResource2012/JHCIRP_POSTbook.pdf.

Grossman, M. (1975). The correlation between health and schooling. In Terleckyz, N. E. (Ed.), *Household Protection and Consumption.* New York: Columbia University.

Houston, D. J. and Richardson, L. E. (2008). Motorcyclist fatality rates and mandatory helmet-use laws. *Accident Analysis and Prevention, 40*(1), 200–208.

Insurance Institute for Highway Safety (IIHS). (2007). Supersport motorcycles are designed for racetracks, driven on highways. *Status Report 42*(9) Special Issues: Motorcycles.

Insurance Information Institute (III). (2016, March 22). Motorcycle crashes. Retrieved from http://www.iii.org/issue-update/motorcycle-crashes.

Insurance Institute for Highway Safety (IIHS). (2016, April 24). Topic: Motorcycles. Retrieved from http://www.iihs.org/iihs/topics/t/motorcycles/topicoverview.

Keeler, T. E. (1994). Highway safety, economic behavior, and driving environment. *American Economic Review, 84*, 684–693.

Lardelli-Claret P., Jimenez-Moleon, J. J., de Dos Luna-del-Castillo, J., Garcıa-Martın, M., Bueno-Cavanillas, A., and Galvez-Vargas, R. (2005). Driver dependent factors and the risk of causing a collision for two wheeled motor vehicles. *Injury Prevention, 11*, 225–231.

Lin, M. R. and Kraus, J. F. (2008). Methodological issues in motorcycle injury epidemiology. *Accident Analysis and Prevention*, *40*(5), 1653-1660.

Lin, M. and Kraus, J. F. (2009) "A review of risk factors and patterns of motorcycle injuries." *Accident Analysis and Prevention*, *41*(4), 710-722.

Long, J. S. (1997). "*Regression models for categorical and limited dependent variables.*" SAGE Publications, Thousands Oaks, CA.

Malyshkina, N. V. and Mannering, F. L. (2010) Empirical assessment of the impact of highway design exceptions on the frequency and severity of vehicle accidents." *Accident Analysis and Prevention, 42*, 131-139.

Mayrose, J. (2008). The effects of a mandatory motorcycle helmet law on helmet use and injury patterns among motorcyclist fatalities. *Journal of Safety Research*, *39*(4), 429-432.

Mergia, W.Y., Eustace, D., Chimba, D. and Qumsiyeh, M., (2013). Exploring factors contributing to injury severity at freeway merging and diverging locations in Ohio. *Accident Analysis and Prevention. 55*, 202-210.

Morris, C. C. 2006. Generalized linear regression analysis of association of universal helmet laws with motorcycle fatality rates. *Accident Analysis and Prevention, 38*(1), 142–147.

Muelleman, R. L., Mlinek, E. J. and Collicott, P. E. (1992). Motorcycle crash injuries and costs: effect of a re-enacted comprehensive helmet-use law. *Annals of Emergency Medicine, 21*, 266–272.

National Center for Statistics and Analysis (NCSA). (2009, June). *Traffic Safety Facts: 2008 Data Motorcycles.* Publication DOT-HS-811-159, Washington, DC.

National Center for Statistics and Analysis (NCSA). (2015, May). Motorcycles: 2013 data. (Traffic Safety Facts. Report No. DOT HS 812 148). Washington, DC: National Highway Traffic Safety Administration.

Pai, C-W., Hwang, K. P. and Saleh, W. (2009) A mixed logit analysis of motorcyclists' right-of-way violation in motorcycle accidents at priority T-junctions. *Accident Analysis and Prevention, 41*, 565-573.

Paulozzi, L. J. (2005). The role of sales of new motorcycles in a recent increase in motorcycle mortality rates. *Journal of Safety Research, 36*(4), 361–364.

Park, H.M. (2009). *Regression models for binary dependent variables using STATA, SAS, and SPSS.* Working paper. Center for Statistical and Mathematical Computing, Indiana University.

Peek-Asa, C., McArthur, D. L. and Kraus, J. F. (1999). The prevalence of non-standard helmet use and head injuries among motorcycle riders. *Accident Analysis and Prevention, 31*(3), 229–233.

Pickrell, T. M. and Stames, M. (2008). *An Analysis of Motorcycle Helmet Use in Fatal Crashes.* Pub. DOT HS 811 011. Washington, DC: National Highway Traffic Safety Administration.

Pickrell, T. M. and Liu, C. (2014, March). Motorcycle Helmet Use in 2013—Overall Results. (Traffic Safety Facts Research Note. Report No. DOT HS 812 010). Washington, DC: National Highway Traffic Safety Administration

Rutledge, R. and Stutts, J. (1993). The association of helmet use with the outcome of motorcycle crash injury when controlling for crash/injury severity. *Accident Analysis and Prevention, 25*(3), 347-353.

Savolainen, P. and Mannering, F. (2007). Probabilistic models of motorcyclists' injury severities in single- and multi-vehicle crashes. *Accident Analysis and Prevention, 39*(5), 955-963.

Savolainen, P.T., Mannering, F.L., Lord, D. and Quddus, M.A. (2011). The statistical analysis of highway crash-injury severities: a review and assessment of methodological alternatives. *Accident Analysis and Prevention, 43*, 1666-1676.

Shaheed, M. and Dissanayake, S. (2011). Risk factors associated with motorcycle crash severity in Kansas. In 90th Annual Meeting of the Transportation Research Board, Washington, DC.

Shaheed, M. S. B., Gkritza, K. and Marshall, D. (2012). Motorcycle conspicuity: what factors have the greatest impact. Ames, IA: Center for Transportation Research and Education, Iowa State University

Shaheed, M. S. B., Gkritza, K., Zhang, W. and Hans, Z. (2013). A mixed logit analysis of two-vehicle crash severities involving a motorcycle. *Accident Analysis and Prevention, 61*, 119-128.

Shankar, V. and Mannering, F. (1996). An exploratory multinomial logit analysis of single-vehicle motorcycle accident severity. *Journal of Safety Research, 27* (3), 183-194.

Shankar, V. and Varghese, C. (2006). *Recent trends in fatal motorcycle crashes*." Pub. HS 810-606. Washington, DC: National Highway Traffic Safety Administration.

Soderstorm, C. A., Dischinger, P. S., Ho, S. M. and Soderstorm, M. T. (1993). Alcohol use, driving records, and crash culpability among injured motorcycle drivers. *Accident Analysis and Prevention, 25*, 711–716.

Teoh, E. R. and Campbell, M. (2010). Role of motorcycle type in fatal motorcycle crashes. *Journal of safety research, 41*(6), 507-512.

Wang, X. and Abdel-Aty, M. (2008). Analysis of left-turn severity by conflicting pattern using partial proportional odds models. *Accident Analysis and Prevention, 40*, 1674-1682.

Wang, Z., Chen, H. and Lu, J.J. (2009). Exploring impacts of factors contributing to injury severity at freeway diverge areas. *Transportation Research Record, 2102*, 43-52.

Wells, S., Mullin, B., Norton, R., Langley, J., Connor, J., Jackson, R. and Lay-Yee, R. (2004). Motorcycle rider conspicuity and crash related injury: case-control study. *Bmj, 328*(7444), 857.

Williams, A. F., Ginsburg, M. J. and Burchman, P. F. (1979). Motorcycle helmet use in relation to legal requirements. *Accident Analysis and Prevention,11*(4), 271-273.

Williams, R., (2006). Generalized ordered logit/partial proportional odds models for ordinal response variables. *The Stata Journal, 6*, 58-82.

Wilson, D. C. (1990). The Effectiveness of Motorcycle Helmets in Preventing Fatalities. Mathematical Analysis Division, NRD-31, March 1989. *Journal of Safety Research, 21*(1), 42.

INDEX

F

G

H

I

L

M

N

O

P

R

S

T

U

V

W

Y